NURTURING Your
CHILD With MUSIC

JOHN M. ORTIZ, PH.D.

NURTURING Your CHILD With MUSIC

How Sound Awareness Creates Happy, Smart and Confident Children

Newleaf

Newleaf
an imprint of
Gill & Macmillan Ltd
Hume Avenue
Park West
Dublin 12
with associated companies throughout the world
www.gillmacmillan.ie

First published in the USA by Beyond Words Publishing Inc, Oregon
© John M. Ortiz 1999
0 7171 30800

Printed by ColourBooks Ltd, Dublin

A catalogue record for this book is available from the British Library.

1 3 5 4 2

This one is for the babies:
Angelique, Anthony-Lucas, Dylan, Jacquie, Jeanna,
Knikee, and—but of course—Michael.

ACKNOWLEDGMENTS

Para mima, a quien tanto le debo. Por tenerme, y quererme,
y dejarme ser quien soy.
Por tocarme su musica, y dejarme oir la mia.
Te quiero por todo.

Roz, for holding my hand and never letting go, and
for listening, listening... and listening.

And Cindy, for listening, and hearing that the
child in me has lots to share.

CONTENTS

SOUND AWARENESS

Music and Sound as Anchor and Sail

Even before my birth, my parents began to nurture my musical development. Although no one in our immediate family had any formal musical training, our home was always an informal training ground for developing musical awareness.

Expecting her first child, my mom found music a nurturing and indispensable ally. Chopin's nocturnes and Mozart's string concertos were particularly effective in soothing her during periods of concern or uneasiness. A homemaker, she found that popular, modern music helped her to pass the time, and kept her happy and optimistic. A natural artist and talented painter, she also found that music helped to stimulate her creativity, and so Mozart, Chopin, and popular tunes all found their way into the colorful tapestries and cheery, hand-painted decorations that awaited my arrival into her musical universe.

My father was an opera man. Little did he know that as he serenaded Mom with his strong, sonorous voice, his loving vibrations were also bringing me the message that the world I was coming into was a safe and astonishing place.

And so I was born into music. My primary recollections of earliest childhood are of my mother singing, lulling me to sleep with her gentle, melodious voice. In fact, the first notation she wrote in my baby book reads,

> *"My darling little boy seems to love music above all other things. Although busier and more active than I had anticipated, he quiets instantly when music is played, turning his head in the direction of the radio or phonograph. His breathing relaxes and he smiles at me, as if thanking me for turning it on for him."*

My father imparted his own musical legacy by way of a distinctive, gliding five-note melody he whistled when he arrived home from work. That simple musical code became a bond between father and son, and left such a strong impression on me that, eighteen years after his passing, the recollection of it still evokes the hope that he'll come walking through the front door, just one more time.

Years before "Surround Sound," I was wrapped in and nourished by it. Whether in the form of encouraging words and praise, or rhythms and melodies, nurturing sounds were part of our family. Soft music was as constant at the dinner table as bread and water, and lively, spirited tunes accompanied us on our Sunday outings, during which we sang, laughed, and shared personal stories. Every family reunion, and there were many, readily escalated into festive singing, dancing, and musical merrymaking—with family, friends, and relatives all taking part in makeshift combos that transformed pots, pans, glassware, and utensils into distinct rhythm instruments. Indifferent to actual song lyrics and proper dance steps, children of all ages joined in unrestricted play. As grandparents and toddlers, mothers and sons, fathers and daughters, and close and distant cousins danced together, family bonds became stronger, and traditions were passed down and across generations. In my reality, that was what families were all about.

In the early sixties, following the turmoil and upheaval of the revolution in our homeland, my family made a hasty exodus from Cuba to the United States, a country filled with language, sounds, and rhythms distinctly different from our own. Faced with this difficult, unprecedented journey, Mom and Dad somehow remained outwardly positive and optimistic, consistently shielding my sisters and me from the emotional pain and cultural isolation they were experiencing. Through words of loving reassurance and a keen, attentive ear to our needs, they focused on harmony over dissonance, turning the transition to our new world into a positive, almost magical adventure. Throughout the process, music—our seventh family member—would not be left behind.

For our first Christmas in this new country, Mom and Dad had saved enough money to buy us a record player. Mom, always a fan of "American music," was nonetheless oblivious to what tunes may have been popular at the time. Undaunted, she simply walked into a record store and, with the help of a clerk, purchased as many of the top "45s" as the family budget allowed. Come Christmas morning, my sisters and I were amazed by how Mom had magically come up with so many of our current favorite records. So aware was she of music as essential to our family fabric that, even during this difficult transitional stage, filled with myriad concerns and responsibilities, it remained a priority. Music, the universal language, provided a powerful ally that helped our parents ease our personal and emotional passage, while introducing us to an exciting world of new social and cultural rhythms.

When the Beatles invaded the United States a few months later, their effect on me was overwhelming. I was still struggling to learn the English language when they arrived, and I interpreted their exotic looks, thick Liverpool accents, and resounding "Yeah, Yeah, Yeah!"— which, to me, sounded like "Yah, Yah!"—as being German. This didn't sound like English to me, and for a few days I thought I now had two new languages to learn. "Meet the Beatles" was the first album I ever bought, and over the next few months the bands that made up the bulk of the original British invasion were instrumental in teaching the English language to a young Cuban boy growing up in southern Virginia. To this day, very few people can figure out exactly where my accent comes from.

Two years later my grandparents gave me one of the greatest Christmas gifts of my life, an electric guitar. The next Christmas, our parents bought our first family stereo, replacing the old record player and continuing a rich tradition of expanding our musical awareness through musical instruments, tape recorders, and countless records and tapes—and later, CDs. It's a tradition that my sisters and I have enthusiastically kept alive. Each new instrument or song, it seems, brings forth a new opportunity to expand our musical horizons and to raise our sound awareness.

At fourteen, I wrote my first song, immortalizing me in my own eyes and introducing fresh avenues for self-therapy and countless opportunities for expressing and expanding my creativity. Twenty-five years later I successfully defended my doctoral dissertation, which supported the findings that—among other things—music does in fact help people to feel more relaxed, more comfortable, and closer to one another. This is something that, apparently, my parents always knew.

During those years between my first song and my graduate studies, I learned that music was a very effective, soothing, inspirational, and grounding force for many people. Much of the world, it seemed, shared my passion, as music's effects were apparent almost everywhere. While studying psychology in college, I realized that my three primary interests—music, psychology, and working with children—could easily be merged and developed into a career. Over the next twenty years, my career path evolved from working with children, teens, and families at state and family agencies and a private school, to developing a private practice. The knowledge and experience I acquired during those years gave me ample opportunities for research and provided a solid clinical foundation that led to my development of Sound Psychology. In Sound Psychology—a combination of traditional psychological techniques, music, and transpersonal concepts—I had developed an approach that greatly facilitated my work with children and adults.

I have been fortunate to see how my Sound Psychology approaches and ideas have made a significant difference in my vocation as a psychologist. In my work with children and adolescents especially, music offers a natural, creative tool through which relationships can be established, developed, and expanded. Used as an "icebreaker" and relationship enhancer in combination with traditional psychological approaches, music helps children open up many worlds of possibilities. They feel more at ease in session, and look forward to return visits, as they begin to experience positive differences in their lives.

As musical awareness grows, affecting and influencing our society, music becomes an increasingly powerful and beneficial ally in my clinical and consulting work. Just as music is used in business and industry to influence minds and sell products, it can be used in counseling and therapy—as well as in schools and in homes—to help motivate, comfort, and support children.

In my first book, *The Tao of Music: Sound Psychology*, I introduced the concepts and techniques of Sound Psychology in a practical, reader-friendly, adult format. That book was designed to help adults raise their "sound awareness"—to show how each of us can use music and sound to change and improve our lives. In this book, I have drawn from my years of research and experience to present a guide for parents—to help them access these positive, timely, "sound awareness" approaches to strengthening bonds, developing family harmony, and nurturing their children.

RAISING SOUND EXPOSURE

Well before children begin to utter decipherable words, parents can introduce them to the essence of communication and social relationships by supporting and encouraging their rapidly developing language-making skills. Because awareness of music and its elements (rhythm, pitch, timbre) develops at about the same rate as speech, music can serve as a powerful ally in the development of sound awareness and language skills. The speed at which young children memorize nursery rhymes, television jingles, and popular tunes illustrates the benefits of combining music and verbal or nonverbal languages. By helping us to relax, pace ourselves, focus, and clear our minds of distracting thoughts, music can help all of us—adults as well as children—to more readily memorize large amounts of information. Once we've acquired this information, musical elements such as tempo, melody, and rhythm make it easier for us to later retrieve and recognize not only the songs and their lyrics, but also the events and feelings that have become associated with the music.

A powerful force that is commonly taken for granted, music can be consciously used to serve many purposes. It can be used as a motivator or a reward for chores completed and responsibilities met. It can be very effective academically by helping to structure learning, reduce boredom, and block out bothersome external noises (or internal thought chatter). It can help manage time by setting a desired pace. By stimulating thoughts, activating emotions, and eliminating awkward silences, music helps to inspire social conversation, helping us to build and develop relationships.

The sheer act of listening to music, in fact, has been found to significantly improve general listening skills, increase attention, and promote expression of thoughts and feelings. By invigorating our personal resources and urging forward movement, music can help us to feel more energetic and confident, enhancing our self-esteem and helping us to look at ourselves, and the world, a little more positively and optimistically. When other things fail, and friends or family are not around, music can help us chase away the blues, let go of anger, unfurl stress, and reduce fear and anxiety. It can lull us to sleep, and even minimize physical pain for periods of time. It gives us a great excuse to sing, dance, or just act silly!

RAISING SOUND AWARENESS:
PURPOSE, GOALS, AND DEFINITIONS

The purpose of this book is to provide a guide through which parents and other caregivers* can more effectively nurture their children by raising, or cultivating, their sound awareness.

The term "sound awareness" is used in this book to describe our ability to tune in to sounds and vibrations that resonate inside us, as well as those that reach us from our surrounding environments. Some of these internal "sounds" include our thoughts; messages related to feelings; "echoes" from our memories; personal interpretations of the sounds and voices we hear; expectations; hopes and wishes; needs and desires. External sounds that affect us include messages from the media and other communication sources; nature sounds; industrial noises; music and songs; and all of the different cultural, ethnic and regional accents, rhythms and voice inflections of the people we encounter from day to day.

The phrase "raising sound awareness" refers to our ability to enhance the ways by which we tune in to our own developing rhythms and tempos, and learn to compose our own harmony, diminishing our dissonance with ourselves or our environments.

---

*The word "parents" is used throughout this book to mean not only parents, but also any other caregivers involved in nurturing children. Although primarily designed for family-related activities, many of the techniques and concepts introduced will prove just as helpful to teachers, counselors, therapists, and any other individuals who work with, or care for, children.

By helping to raise our sound awareness, the goal of this book is to help all family members, parents and their children, to become better able to tune in to healthy and positive vibrations and enjoy more fulfilling, happy, smart, and confident lives.

HOW TO USE THIS BOOK

This book is designed as a hands-on, practical guide that parents can turn to when searching for creative musical alternatives to nurture their children. It is primarily intended for children age "zero" (i.e., still in the womb!) through age twelve. Each section is broken into four general areas (infants, toddlers, preschoolers, school-age children) to enable parents to access relevant exercises and suggestions while focusing on their own children's specific developmental needs.

Parents can scan the table of contents and choose from among dozens of sections that provide original ideas for raising sound awareness, as well as games and techniques through which they can support and nourish their children's developing needs. Having chosen a specific area to focus on, they may then select from among various exercises and "sound suggestions" which are accompanied by brief instructions in a simple step-by-step format designed to make daily life situations and events more fun, positive, educational, and enriching. Once a particular exercise or suggestion is selected, parents may then turn to one or more of the thirty-one "Music Menus" included either at the end of relevant chapters, or in Appendix A. Here, they will find hundreds of recommended titles that help to complement each section, or to create desired moods and environments.

THE MUSIC MENUS

The hundreds of choices included throughout the thirty-one Music Menus in this book were carefully selected from both classic and currently popular children's titles, and then placed into relevant sections to help parents choose specific types of music to meet specific goals. Starting with selections for babies still in their prenatal stage, the menus include lists of tunes that range from helping children to develop their academic skills, raising self-esteem and exercising, to relaxing, getting to sleep, improving communication and listening skills, or just enjoying themselves. The menus are presented as *suggestions* for parents to consider when sorting through the thousands of titles available in today's rapidly growing market. In the end, parents must consider a number of factors—such as their children's preferences, and family budget—before deciding which titles may be most appropriate for their own children, and for meeting individual needs.

Finally, as most parents know, adult personal needs must often wait until after the children are well taken care of. Following suit, this book's final section is designed for parents—to remind them that, as they work to compose family harmony, they must also fine-tune themselves.

THE TIME FACTOR

Because parents are busy people, this book was designed to maximize the benefits that can be gained from music and sound, while minimizing the amount of time parents need to invest to profit from these techniques and ideas. Available time varies greatly from person to person and day to day. What may be reasonable for one person may seem overwhelming to another. With that in mind, here are some suggestions parents may consider to maximize this book's effectiveness.

- Read the introduction, which describes the book's goals and purposes, and acquaint yourself with the different sections by reading the table of contents.
- Start with one area that particularly interests you or your child, and go from there. (One of the benefits of a book such as this is that it is designed so that each chapter stands on its own—you can "skip around.") After reading the introduction, turn to any chapter you like, or one you feel may address a particular need (relaxation, self-esteem, sleeping, language development, listening skills, stimulation, and so on).
- Wherever you begin, and whichever direction you take in your sound explorations, you will improve with time and practice. The book provides many ideas for self-reminders to help you, and

your children, stay "sound aware" (or, "aware of sound") throughout the course of a typical day.

How much time should you spend on any one activity? One of the
book's purposes is to raise our awareness of how much we take sound
(music included) for granted. To remedy that, the book is filled with
exercises, ideas and examples of things that we can do to teach our
children—and ourselves—to "tune in" to these sounds and use them to
our advantage. Ranging from simple things such as paying attention to
our voice tone (which can be done any time you speak with someone),
to playing soft music during dinner (once in a while, or as a supper-
time tradition), to embarking on weekly "Sound Safaris" (see chapter
9), the book presents hundreds of options to choose from that can be
tailored to fit any time budget. The responsibility and decisions—as
well as the fun and enrichment—are all yours! To further assist parents, however, some sample "sound awareness" days are provided in
Appendix C (see "A Musical Day in the Life of...").

THE APPENDICES

This book includes well-researched appendices aimed at making
families' sound adventures a little easier. Additional general Music
Menus are included here, which contain both specific and general
recommendations parents can consider for many of the text's exercises. The music selections are divided into various categories to
simplify the choice-making process. In addition, Music Menu 28, "A
Quick Glossary of Popular Musical Styles," provides a brief overview of
forty of the most currently popular musical styles and genres, from
Alternative and Ambient through Techno to World. Lists of music
organizations, general resource materials, and recommended
research sources are also provided.

CLINICALLY SOUND AND RESEARCH-BASED

The concepts, techniques, and suggestions provided throughout this
book are based on more than twenty years of professional clinical and

consulting experience, and gathered through working with thousands of families, extending across a wide spectrum of cultural, regional, and ethnic populations. The book also draws from a vast sample of textbooks, scientific research journals, and current parenting publications to provide parents and their children with scientifically based recommendations that strive to bring together modern ideas and traditional family values.

This book is not intended as a panacea, or as a universal remedy for all family problems or situations. Furthermore, parents are reminded that the exercises and suggestions recommended throughout the book will not work equally well for all children in all situations. Parents are encouraged to exercise their right to choose and use the types of music they feel will most adequately fit their family goals, belief systems, and lifestyles. In the end, as most parents recognize, regardless of how good any concept or technique may appear to be, there is no substitute for active personal involvement, positive nurturing relationships, and unconditional love.

1

BEFORE THE BABY
Music for the Prenatal Experience

Be aware: sound awareness begins before birth. As a line to a popular song goes, "the rhythm's gonna get ya," apparently even in the womb! Babies in utero, scientists have found, begin to react to both internal body sounds and to sounds from outside the womb as early as the fourth or fifth month of development.

Providing music and other pleasant sounds for unborn babies has been found to stimulate their auditory systems and to have a positive effect on their response to music and other sounds after birth. Babies exposed to soothing, relaxing music while in the womb have also been found to grow and gain weight easily, and to be more at peace with themselves and their environment once they are welcomed into the "real world."

A MOTHER'S VOICE

Studies consistently indicate that fetuses are far more in tune with their mothers' voices than with any other voices or sounds coming from the outside environment. Without exception, each mother-to-be with whom I've consulted has indicated that her baby not only responded to external music, but behaved differently depending on the volume and the type of music being played. These reactions, which are supported by research findings on heart-rate differences, are also apparently more pronounced when the mothers engage in singing, playing a musical instrument, or listening to their favorite types of music.

When I was born, my mom had just turned sixteen. She was herself alienated and estranged from her friends and family, who convinced her that her only option was to recognize she had made a mistake, put me up for adoption, and "forget about it." She named me Marshall and, as I found out years later, she sang and spoke to me from the moment she knew I was kicking inside her until I was formally adopted by a loving, caring couple a few weeks after my birth. My adoptive parents were very open with me from the beginning, telling me that I was adopted and about the circumstances under which my mom had been forced to let me go, never to see me again. I never felt comfortable calling them "Mom and Dad" and so always addressed them by their first names.

One night, when I myself was sixteen, I was in my room playing a video game with two of my friends. Completely involved and absorbed in the game, I suddenly heard a voice from behind calling out my name, "Marshall?" Instinctively, without any conscious thought whatsoever, I turned around and answered, "Mom?" and there she was in the room with me. It was the first time I recall ever saying that word, "Mom."

—Marshall, twenty-eight, composer

SOOTHING SOUNDS: THE (HEART)BEAT GOES ON

So, with our twenty-first century technology already lending evidence to what most of us have suspected all along (that music can be a pretty wonderful thing!), how can mothers use this knowledge to their advantage? More specifically, what can mothers do to help raise the sound awareness of their babies during the process of becoming? The following suggestions are offered to help mothers benefit from the power of music and sound while also sharing these healthful vibrations with their babies.

Read. Babies who are read the same stories by their mothers two or three times a day, for six to eight weeks before birth, seem to be familiar with and highly receptive to these stories once they are born. Mothers may choose from among the many current, and classic, collections of children's stories, poems and rhyming books widely available—but at this stage of a child's development, of course, the material itself is not as important as selecting readings that you find pleasant and simple to read, and that you will enjoy sharing with your child.

Relax. Set aside two or three twenty-minute periods during which you retire to a quiet spot, lie down, close your eyes and surrender to your favorite soothing, meditative sounds or music. Familiar sounds, particularly those that both Mom and baby can learn to associate with rest and relaxation, can be played after the baby's arrival to help soothe and calm the newborn child. Every gentle breath you take will help to send the message that the world your baby is about to enter is a safe place.

Listen. The music mothers listen to, particularly during the final trimester, seems to be most effective in later getting newborn babies' attention, as well as in helping to stimulate or comfort them. Mothers are encouraged to select tunes from among their own musical favorites. Most adults living in Europe and North America prefer Western, consonant music that follows a steady pulse, and so do their babies. Music by Baroque composers such as Bach, Vivaldi, Corelli, Telemann, Scarlatti, Pachelbel, and Handel; some New Age music; and Mozart's beautiful melodies all appear to be quite effective. Newborn babies also seem to enjoy music-box tunes, lullabies, and children's songs, especially when they are performed in the mother's native language.

Play favorite tunes. Surrounding yourself as often as possible with the music you find soothing, relaxing, and peaceful provides sound vibrations that will positively affect your unborn baby, with the double advantage of helping you to relax and directly pass on your own feelings of relaxation to your baby.

When a need for stimulation and alertness beckons, expose yourself to music that has moderately upbeat, steady rhythms. This will help to stimulate the baby as well. Volume should be kept at a modest, "middle of the road" level.

Follow your heart. Most babies are soothed by the sound and pulse of a moderately relaxed (sixty-eight to seventy-two beats per minute) heartbeat. Mothers of newborn babies using sound machines that provide an artificial heartbeat sound consistently report that the constant, rhythmic pulse is extremely effective in helping to calm their children, even helping them to fall asleep quite readily. Research not only supports these observations but also indicates that this exposure to soothing heartbeat sounds promotes weight gain among these more relaxed, peaceful babies.

Play an instrument. Playing an instrument is yet another method for sharing sounds and positive vibrations with your unborn baby. If there is an instrument you've wanted to take up, this may be the last chance you get for a while! Concentrating on playing an instrument helps our minds to take "mini vacations" from life's ordeals, giving us a chance to use a different part of our brains while the overworked part takes a break. Also, playing an instrument will help you to focus, relax, and add pleasant stimulation to your sound environment. If at all possible, take up an instrument and learn to play. Many musician parents say their unborn babies become more animated when they play their instruments. The vibrations you receive from your instrument will travel inward, massaging you—as well as your baby— while cultivating a love and understanding of music from yet another perspective.

Speak and sing to your baby. Fetuses have been found to be particularly receptive to the human voice. Newborn babies readily orient themselves to their mothers' voices.

Hum, chant, tone. Humming, chanting, or toning warm, soothing sounds is an excellent way to give yourself and your baby an "internal massage." Pregnant women often report that their babies seem quieter when they sing, hum, chant, or tone.

Whistle happy tunes. Fetuses respond most actively to rhythm and pitch. Whistling can provide a rainbow of vibrational samplings, introducing your baby to a universe of diverse auditory delights.

Promote sound awareness among the whole family. Dad can hum, sing, or whistle *his* favorite tunes so that Daddy's voice and vibrations become as familiar as Mommy's. If there are other children in the family, they can sing *their* favorite songs or rhymes to their new brother or sister, so that the new baby becomes pleasantly attuned to their voices.

Exposure to different types of sounds—the parents' voices, voice tones, and accents; particular tunes—will help to increase your child's sensitivity to and familiarity with these vibrations after birth. As a result, the musical diet you feed your unborn child will continue to resonate for many years to come.

In summary, the verdict from satisfied mothers, which is supported by many research studies, is that the music Mom plays, listens to, and sings during pregnancy will go a long way in shaping the lifetime musical preferences and personal sound awareness of her child.

Music Menu #1
Sound resources* recommended for nurturing the baby and mother-to-be

Love Chords	Thomas Verny and Sandra Collier
Sound and Spirit: Welcoming Children Into the World	Various artists
Transitions:** Maternal and Fetal Wellness Program	Burt and Joe Wolff
Transitions: Womb Sounds for Mother and Child	and Dr. Fred Schwartz

Music Menu #2
Popular children's music companies and artists

New parents may find it hard to sort out the thousands of children's music titles that are available in the market. The following menu is provided to introduce new parents to some of the more popular current companies and artists in today's children's music arena.

---

*Unless otherwise specified, the sound resources recommended throughout this book refer to CD and/or audio-cassette format. Some, but not all, titles may be available in both formats.

**"Transitions" is the name of a series of recordings, based on scientific research, which were specifically designed for infants and which utilize actual womb sounds to relax and ease babies into sleep.

Popular children's music companies:

American Heroes and Legends	Storybook Classics
Kimbo Educational	Amazing Animals
Disney	Sesame Street
AudioBook	Dr. Seuss
Kidsongs	Rock 'N Learn
Wee Sing	Winnie the Pooh

Popular children's artists:

Barney	Marc Brown
Ella Jenkins (Folkways/Smithsonian)	Raffi
Joanie Bartels	Marc Brown
Linda Arnold	Bill Harley
Hap Palmer	Odds Bodkin
Jim Weiss	Charlotte Diamond
Greg and Steve	Richard Scarry
Twin Sisters	

2

MUSIC AND LANGUAGE ACQUISITION

The purpose of this chapter is to briefly discuss how speech and language develop, and to provide some sound tools that parents may consider in assisting their children as they make the transitions from preverbal through verbal stages of development.

For whatever reason, music was just not a very important commodity in our home when we were growing up. It wasn't until my teens that I realized that, outside of church hymns on Sundays, music was essentially missing from our family picture. From that point on, however, music became truly important in my life and I haven't looked back since. In fact, one of the most difficult decisions Ben and I had to make for our wedding involved choosing our theme song. Since then, we've been experimenting with all different types of music, figuring out things like what songs seem to help which moods at different times.

Our kids seem to have really benefited from our "musical experiments." When Kyle, our oldest boy, was just short of two, I started to involve him as much as possible in singing, listening to songs and playing with musical instruments. One of the things I did with him was sit down and teach him songs. He was just learning to speak then, but he could sing those songs! Whenever he'd mispronounce a certain word in the song, or try to get around it, I would make up little games where we would go back to that word and he would repeat it with different inflections and tones of voice. We'd sing the same line several times throughout the day and I would then use it in different phrases and talk about the meaning of the word. We couldn't believe the positive difference this made in his overall pronunciation and the effect it seemed to have on his focusing on language in general. Later, we did the same thing with his younger brother and sister but started out

even earlier. By the time each of them reached kindergarten,
their teachers raved about how advanced their speech and
vocabularies were.

—Stephanie, housewife, thirty-four

From the moment of birth, newborns begin to collect personal "auditory blueprints," assembling the phonemes and other sounds spoken by those around them. In this manner, babies exposed to different languages such as Chinese, French, and English will develop a number of different neural connections that will assist them in fluently speaking what will be their native tongues. By about the age of one, recent research shows, those blueprints are pretty much set, and the learning and reproduction of foreign sounds becomes increasingly more difficult. Exposing children to many diverse sounds (words, music, and sounds in general) during this first year, therefore, stimulates their brains to form many different types of "sound connections," clearing the way for expanded sound repertoires later in life. Early exposure to different types of music has been found to increase the diversity, flexibility, and endurance of those neural connections, particularly in areas of math, language, and logic.

Language involves words and their pronunciation, and the ways in which they can be combined to express feelings and ideas to others. Both verbal and nonverbal, language includes sounds, gestures, and signs, and any number of different dialects, idioms, jargons, styles, and expressions. Speech, on the other hand, involves the use of language to communicate or express feelings and ideas through audible words. Speech is "language out loud," verbal interaction, conversation. Music, whether vocal, instrumental, electronic or mechanical, involves the ordering of tones and sounds in time, using different sequences and combinations of rhythm, melody, and/or harmony. Language, speech, and music can each be shared, expressed, or received through speaking or singing, listening, reading and writing, and composing.

With a little forethought and imagination, parents can expose their infants to a vast universe of desirable sounds and musical styles, encouraging both listening and efforts at creative sound imitations.

The processes of listening to and creating music and nurturing sounds provide a number of advantages for both preverbal and verbal children by:

· Enhancing listening skills.
· Setting the groundwork for language development and voice dynamics.
· Introducing the voice as an instrument.
· Teaching how to interpret a person's emotional state (e.g., sad, happy, relaxed, excited) through vocal qualities such as pitch, tone, and volume.
· Sharpening focusing and attention skills.
· Developing a sense of rhythm, harmony, tempo, and anticipation.
· Providing nonverbal ways of communicating.
· Functioning as a nurturing bridge that escorts children as they develop their vocabularies and learn new ways of self-expression.
· Furnishing a means through which children can begin to structure sound by way of repetitive patterns, rhythmic schemes, and continuous beats that help to set and maintain steady tempos.
· Increasing comfort with organized, purposeful, and controlled behaviors.
· Stimulating a sense of alertness.
· Contributing an outlet for channeling energy throughout the entire developmental spectrum, from gurgling to singing, bouncing to dancing, and hopping to aerobics.
· Affording a means through which children can relate to their peers, thereby helping them to develop both self and group images, communication styles, and social skills.
· Helping to develop auditory memory and discrimination.

PREVERBAL TO VERBAL LANGUAGE DEVELOPMENT

Although theories that attempt to explain how speech, language, and musical abilities are acquired and developed vary, there is substantial agreement suggesting that all three of these abilities evolve at very similar rates.

The following views are among those most commonly accepted.

Genetic: the "I was born this way!" theory. The genetic view is a neurologically and physiologically based theory proposing that our brains are "programmed" from birth. It suggests that our speech and language capabilities are pre-wired and inherited, and that these skills develop at certain natural rates.

Behavioral: the "you do what you learn, you learn what you do!" theory. The behavioral theory suggests that speech and language are directly and indirectly taught and shaped by parents, siblings and others who *reinforce* the linguistic elements that eventually become our learned language.

Cognitive: the "See it … Know it … Say it!" theory. The cognitive model posits that language and speech patterns develop from mental images and actually follow, rather than lead to, intellectual development.

Other schools of thought suggest that language development involves a combination of two or all three of the above, while also including a number of social, cultural, and other diverse elements. Regardless of which theory parents lean toward, the bottom line is that through support, nurturing, and encouragement, parents can significantly and positively influence their children's ability to learn, use, and appreciate language, music, and other sounds.

DEVELOPING LANGUAGE SKILLS

As can be expected, the development of speech, language, and response to music and other sounds is not an exact science and will vary from individual to individual. Unrealistic expectations can often prove to be quite frustrating for parents and children alike. Although variations occur from child to child, recent research studies indicate that preverbal and verbal vocal development occurring between birth and forty-eight months follows a fairly general sequence.

Birth to one month: Shortly after birth, newborns are capable of distinguishing between different sounds, instinctively searching for their source, attuning to changes in rhythms, and focusing on music in their environment. During this stage infants learn to coordinate and control their breathing patterns. This is primarily a period of producing gurgling and vocal sounds with crying patterns that are rather sporadic and nonspecific.

Two to three months: Cooing and gurgling, including changes in pitch and vowel-type babbling sounds, are prevalent. Crying becomes a means of communication; the infant relies on crying and other sounds to communicate needs and sensations such as pleasure, discomfort, and hunger. At the extreme, some infants are able to duplicate specific sounds, pitch, and volume, and even to sound out melodies sung by their mothers.

Four to six months: This stage is typically a time for vocal play, such as making high-pitched noises, squealing, whispering, and screaming. At this age, already quite selective about their musical and sound preferences, babies are busily bobbing up and down and swaying to the beat of the music. Even at this early age, some infants are capable of copying specific rhythmic patterns in their quest for speech.

Seven to eleven months: "Lalling" (attempts at imitating certain sounds integrated over the first few months) follows rhythmic tempos and includes melodic "singing." This is the beginning of a process during which babies experiment with repetitive vowels and consonants, and which leads to formal speech and singing.

Nine to twelve months: Organized babbling and primitive "words" that show signs of musical ability, creative play, and recognition of familiar tunes are common at this age. Speech imitations and echoing of sounds become more refined but are still at a period of experimentation. During this first-year period, rhythm is the element that has the greater effect on infants, who are often found hopping and bopping to upbeat tunes and rhythmic sounds.

Twelve to eighteen months: Proper single words are uttered intentionally as children begin to grasp melodies, rhythms, and even word fragments from familiar tunes and adult conversation. Pitch becomes more pronounced during the second year, with babies stretching the use of this new "tool" (and often, their parents' tolerance) into new territory.

Eighteen to twenty-four months: Children play creatively with favorite tunes, imitating and anticipating melodies, and attempting to join in when songs are played or sung. The use of language for social communication typically begins sometime during the second year as vocabularies develop and expand at increasingly rapid rates.

Twenty-four to thirty-six months: During their third year, children are typically able to communicate verbally, sing popular tunes and nursery rhymes, repeat jingles, and speak more rhythmically. Spontaneous songs that explore a moderate range of tempos and tones are randomly created, or brought together in pieces from favorite tunes, as children appear to be trying to invent original musical forms. A peak time for fictional action songs and imitative behaviors.

Thirty-six to forty-eight months: A heightened awareness of various sounds (musical and nonmusical), variations in pitch, and "absolute pitch" is further honed around the third or fourth year. Traditional songs shared among peers become the norm, and creative experimentation gives way to more accepted, structured tunes. Although able to use words and duplicate a number of different rhythms without difficulty, some children at this age may continue to struggle with pitch and melodies. At this age, many children are able to begin taking part in musical games that require some coordination of simple body movements. This provides an excellent way for them to learn concepts such as up and down, left and right, and fast and slow.

Although some children, as noted above, can basically match the pitch and melodic forms of certain tunes as early as two or three months of age, others continue to have problems reproducing these sounds as late as their fifth or sixth year. Most children in our western culture, however, are capable of understanding, learning, appreciating, and duplicating popular and traditional tunes by the time they enter the first grade.

By around age four, children have begun to develop a sound musical foundation, expanding and refining their sound-making abilities in many ways.

Ages four through six: By this age, most children are capable of socially interacting and sharing with their peers. They are better able to understand and follow instructions, which makes it possible for them to become more involved in formal musical games such as those that require clapping to a beat, and hopping and skipping in rhythmic movements. Kinesthetic skills are further refined during this period.

Ages seven through ten: Basic motor skills and coordination are refined during these years, enabling children to take part in more structured activities such as formal dancing. Improved fine motor skills increase their ability to play musical instruments. Children at this age are also capable of learning musical notation, as well as memorizing and duplicating more complex rhythms, melodies, and tempos. They are also more apt to sit through a musical performance than children in the four to six age range. Greater involvement in social activities makes these children excellent candidates for organized musical activities such as singing in choirs and playing in school bands, or even small combos. Visual skills are also further refined during this period.

Ages ten through twelve: Increasingly capable of thinking in abstract terms, children can now begin to understand concepts that require imagery and to deal with external, more communal topics. Children in this age group are greatly influenced by peers and media marketing and are busy establishing their own identities. By raising their sound awareness of their children's musical preferences, parents will be able to tune in to their children's personal struggles and explorations, which are often reflected in their musical leanings. Auditory skills are further refined during this period.

Following are a number of suggestions that can help to promote and support sound awareness, as well as language, speech, and the acquisition and development of musical abilities.

Sound Suggestion #1
Follow the leader

Don't hesitate to imitate or mimic your infant's attempts at sound exploration. From the very first coo to the magical first word, your acting as a reflective and unconditionally accepting "sounding board" to your children's loving efforts at speech will help them to stay in tune with their own progress. As your children hear and observe your mimicking of their sounds, you will help to set a foundation for social communication. It will also provide you an early leadership experience.

Sound Suggestion #2
Use sound descriptions

Using creative combinations of various "sound words" and intonations to describe sounds, objects, and actions can be a wonderful way to introduce the notion of sound to your infant while sharing general knowledge. The following exercises provide some ideas to help illustrate this approach to raising sound awareness.

Exercise #1

While variably holding your child high in the air and then low to the ground, for example, you may say, "I'm holding you *high* . . . and now I'm holding you *low*," varying your pitch to illustrate the connection between physical height and tone or sound quality.

Exercise #2

Encourage your infant to touch, stroke, and squeeze various objects; describe each one by name while you embellish your descriptions with sound twists and intonations. For example, while a plush, furry toy may be described as "soft kitty" by using warm and gentle tones, a wooden or metal object may be referred to as "hard chair" by using a firm voice tone.

Sound Suggestion #3

If you can say it you can sing it

Adding simple melody lines and rhythms to your daily interactions will help to stimulate your child's creativity, raise interest in the message you are trying to convey, and activate both the right (artistic, musical) and left (more analytical, language) hemispheres of the brain. Borrowing melody lines from favorite hit tunes, or your child's favorite nursery rhymes, will help you to compensate if you feel you lack natural musical ability! A rhyming dictionary will likewise help to add volumes to your existing repertoire, allowing you to soar beyond those "Cat in the Hat" and "moon in June" rhymes (see page 18 for some recommended nursery rhyme titles).

Other ideas, such as speed, distance, size, texture, and, of course, volume, may also be illustrated by varying voice tone qualities.

Speed: Combining sound descriptions with fast and slow songs and physical activities is an excellent way of illustrating differences in speed. While playing a song with a fast tempo, spin, trot, hop, dance, shake, or otherwise move around the room at a speed reflecting the beat of the song, and say, "We're spinning/dancing/shaking *fast*!" Switching to a slow tune, repeat the exercise once again, but this time use a *s-l-o-w-e-r* tempo and voice inflections to illustrate the differences.

Distance: A "far away" voice can describe a bird or an airplane flying high overhead; mimicking an echo, for example, adds fun and dimension to activities. Imitate the fading sound of a flat stone as it skips over water, a ball bouncing and rolling away, or a bird flying off into the distance ("Look at that bird flying far away...way...way...").

Size: Alternating between "tiny" and "big" voices, hold your child's hand against your own and say, "My hand is *big*...your hand is *small*."

This exercise works well for teaching your child the names of body parts, from toes to head! ("This is your *big* toe . . . and this is your *little* toe . . . this is my *big* foot, and this is your *little* foot. . .")

Texture: Select a few especially soft and smooth, or rough and rugged, garments and, while guiding your child's hand in stroking and feeling the fabrics, use different adjectives and voice tones to make connections between the textural qualities and sounds associated with the different fibers. ("This shirt is *soft* . . . these jeans are *rough*.")

Volume: Select a song of medium tempo. Begin by playing it at a moderate level and say, "This volume sounds just right!" Now raise the volume for a few seconds until it becomes loud enough that you have to raise your voice to say, "This music is too loud!" Lower the volume until the music is barely audible, and use a hushed voice to whisper, "This music is now too quiet!" Raise the volume once again to a moderate level and repeat the sequence a number of times, making sure that you end the exercise by playing the music at a desired level for at least twenty to thirty seconds.

In the end, regardless of whether your purpose is teaching your child the differences between warm and cold, dark and bright, or crunchy and chewy, keep in mind that "sound words" and voice intonations can serve as enriching tools to help broaden and diversify your child's learning experience.

Sound Suggestion #4
Provide musical instruments

Cost will often determine the quality and diversity of the musical instruments parents select for their children. A balanced mix of exploration and perseverance, however, will often lead to a treasure trove of instruments ranging from acceptable to superb in quality. Although great bargains may present themselves when least expected (friends and neighbors, department stores, garage and sidewalk sales) it is unwise to count on the unexpected. A more proactive approach may include searching through bargain bins at musical instrument stores or pawnshops; in music catalogs and classified ads; and on the Internet. (Please see Appendix B for music catalog and Web site suggestions.) Music departments at local schools, colleges, or churches may at times also provide a resource for secondhand instruments as programs are updated, revamped, or, sadly, eliminated. In selecting used or inexpensive instruments for your child, primary concerns should include:

- safety (it's always wise to have used instruments professionally checked out, cleaned, and adjusted),
- clean and functional (and for wind and brass, sanitized) instruments, and,
- rich and tuneful rather than flat, "scratchy," or piercing, brassy sounds.

Following are sound resources recommended for nurturing your child's language development.

Music Menu #3
Music for alphabet and phonics

A to Z, The Animals and Me	Kimbo Educational
ABC's and 123's	Blues Clues
Alphabet Day with Pooh	Disney
Alphabet Zoo	Barney
Alphabet	The Fun-Damentals
Barney's Read-along ABC Animals!	Barney
Can a Jumbo Jet Sing the Alphabet?	Hap Palmer
Various Titles	Clifford Series
Dog Days: Rhymes Around the Year	Jack Prelutsky
Various Titles	Eyewitness Series
Phonics: Consonants and Vowels	Twin Sisters
Sing A to Z	Sharon, Lois and Bram
Sing the Alphabet	Sesame Street
Various Titles (phonics and letter sounds)	Rock 'N Learn

Music Menu #4
Music for developing speech and language

Songs and Rhymes: Fall, Spring, and Winter	Phonemic Awareness
Rhyming Words	The Fun-Damentals
Rhythm and Rhymes	Josh Greenberg
Rhythms of Childhood	Ella Jenkins
Rhythms and Game Songs for Little Ones	Ella Jenkins
Circle Time: Songs and Rhymes for the Very Young	Lisa Monet
Jump Down: Songs and Rhymes for the Very Young	Lisa Monet
The Classroom Collection (box set)	Classical Kids
The Word Factory	Dan Crow
Early Ears (CD collection for children from birth to school age)	Various Artists

Music Menu #5
Nursery rhymes

Baby's Nursery Rhymes	Phylicia Rashad
Classic Nursery Rhymes	Hap Palmer
Humpty Dumpty: 40 Favorite Nursery Rhymes	Storybook Classics
It's Singing Time: A Collection of Nursery Rhymes	Bananas in Pajamas
Nursery Days	Woody Guthrie
Nursery Raps	Natalie Cole
Nursery Rhymes for Little People	Various Artists
Nursery Rhymes	Rock 'N Learn
Rap Rhymes: Mother Goose on the Loose	Various Artists
Wee Sing Nursery Rhymes	Wee Sing

Music Menu #6
Music for learning foreign languages

Barney in Outer Space (Spanish)	Barney
Fun French for Kids	Beth Manners
Fun Spanish for Kids	Beth Manners
Soy Una Pizza (Spanish)	Charlotte Diamond
Spanish, Vols. 1 & 2	Rock 'N Learn
Teach Me Spanish (three volumes)	Teach Me Tapes

My Name Is Cheech, The School Bus Driver	Cheech Marin
Sign & ABCs: A New Way to Play	John Kinstler
(American Sign Language)	and Antoinette Abbamonte
French	Rock 'N Learn
Various languages (French, German, Italian, Spanish)	Twin Sisters
Lyric Language Series: Spanish, French, Italian,	Penton Overseas
Japanese and German	(videos)
Teach Me Tapes: Chinese, French, Spanish, German, Hebrew,	
Italian, Japanese, Russian and English	Teach Me Tapes
Spanish: Esta Es Mi Terra	Jose Luiz Orosco
Spanish: Diez Deditos	Jose Luiz Orosco
Universe of Song (Spanish)	Maria Del Rey

Music Menu #7 ⌊ 9 5, 6 5 0 | 7 8 0 . 8 3

Sing-alongs

All You Need Is Love: Beatles for Kids	Raffi, Eric Bibb and
	child singers
Singable Songs for the Very Young	Raffi
The Singable Songs Collection	Raffi
Pat the Bunny: Sing with Me	Various Artists
One More River	Bill Staines
Little Voices in My Head	Susan Salidor
Timeless	Cathy Block
Disney's Winnie the Pooh Sing-Along	Various Artists
Elmo's Favorite Sing-Along Songs	Sesame Street
The Lion King	Disney Sing-Along
Pocahontas	Disney Sing-Along
Peanut Butter & Jelly's Greatest Hits	Tom Knight & Liz McMahon
Yellow Submarine: A Songtrack	The Beatles

A, E, I, O, U: THE ABC'S OF MUSICAL AWARENESS

Although most infants demonstrate some degree of natural musical ability from very early on, the range of aptitude depends on many factors. Among other things, these may include genetics, the amount of music in the household (such as parents' singing and playing instruments and recorded music), and even the extent of parents' formal musical training.

Suzuki: a structured approach. The following description of the world-renowned Suzuki approach is given to provide an example of a highly structured music education program.

The Suzuki method of talent education through music provides an excellent—albeit extreme—example of how early, and effectively, proficiency in musical performance can be taught and developed in children. Children involved in this program begin their training at age one, at which time they listen daily to selected recordings of great performances. At around age two, the children and their mothers, who are very highly involved in the program, begin to attend group music lessons that include games and formal exercises. Emphasis is placed on each child's progress, and competition is discouraged. The mothers and teachers play very active roles, constantly encouraging and motivating the children, acting as inspirational as well as practical coaches as the children learn to play selected pieces of music. Once the children's excitement and interest in playing the instrument are maximized, they are finally given the opportunity to begin lessons on their own instruments. Mothers and children begin to practice together and follow a strict curriculum during which the children's progress and motivation are carefully monitored and encouraged; the mothers' involvement in the lessons gradually diminishes and eventually ends.

Although emphasis is placed on the constant improvement and sharpening of musical skills, challenges are presented carefully and positively so as not to discourage or frustrate the children. This program has been found to be so effective that even students of average musical talent are able to play complicated classical musical pieces before adolescence. Still, rather than having as its purpose the making of young virtuosos, the essence of this method—according to its founders—is the use of music, discipline, and encouragement to maximize children's abilities, build positive self-concepts and strong character, and enhance their belief in themselves.

In spite of the enormous success and wonderful benefits of the Suzuki method and other formal training programs, many children and parents may not be cut out for—or necessarily interested in—such a structured and intensive approach. With that in mind, what can parents do to help maximize their children's musical potential, levels of proficiency, and musical awareness?

Less structured approaches. The following story illustrates how a typical family naturally and instinctively made musical awareness a part of their daily lives, creating a tradition that spanned and enriched several generations.

The earliest musical recollection I have, and it's a strong one, dates back to a wooden music box my grandmother had that played "The Blue Danube." To this day I never hear that tune without smelling Grandma's raisin-bran cookies and seeing her smiling face. Beyond that, I clearly recall Mom singing my sisters Daisy and Grace and me to sleep with lullabies every night, and Dad struggling through the nursery rhymes he played on his guitar, which to us was sort of like a magic wand.

In fact, most of my early family memories have some sort of music association. Every house had its own soundtrack. Grandpa (Dad's dad) loved Big Band music, especially Glenn Miller, and Grandma was always singing old gospels. Ma and Pa (Mom's parents) always had classical music resonating through the house, usually piano pieces by Liszt and Rachmaninoff, they really liked the heavy stuff! Back at our own house Mom introduced me to lighter classical and rock music. Bach and Handel are still her favorites, but she also loves 50s and 60s rhythm and blues. As far as Dad goes, it's hard to imagine him not whistling some tune, usually because, although he has a pretty good voice, he hardly ever knows the lyrics to anything! Dad was the first among our circle of friends' parents to have an eight-track, then a cassette, and then a CD player in his car, so everyone always thought of him as a pretty cool guy. Everyone in our house went to sleep and woke up to a different radio station, it really helped to set the pace, whether it

*was to slow us down to sleep, or alert us to the day. Dinner music
was usually something soft and mellow like Brahms, Debussy or
Mendelssohn.*

*But the most fun was the car trips, pop songs in five-part har-
mony, with Dad making up words to half the songs. John and I
have three daughters ourselves now, and our family soundtrack is
pretty much a tapestry of all the above.*

—Cathy, thirty-six, dance teacher

The following general suggestions and exercises are meant as an
overview of some basic ideas that parents may consider for raising
their child's musical awareness. More specialized areas, guidelines,
and recommendations are offered throughout the book.

Exercise #1
Raising musical awareness

Step 1. During your child's early infancy, focus on the parent-child relationship and allow your baby to "be" musical; set an example by
providing musical environments in your home. Sing, play an instrument, play recorded music, rent musicals and watch them as a family.

Step 2. Make musical instruments available to your older children. They
make great birthday and holiday gifts. Acoustic or electronic keyboards,
simple string (inexpensive guitars, ukuleles) and wind (flutes, horns)
instruments, and percussion (drums, bells, chimes) instruments cover
a fairly wide musical spectrum and can be a safe investment that fits
most budgets. Once your child begins to show an inclination in one
area or another, accommodations can be made and quality instruments
considered. Current studies strongly indicate that rich musical environments and ongoing support and encouragement appear to be greater
predictors of later musical ability and achievement than innate or
"natural" talent. Once your children show an interest in particular
instruments you may want to encourage music classes.

Step 3. Become a musical role model; take up an instrument (or revive
an old one) and hold joint practice sessions. There can be no greater
show of support for your children than personal involvement.

Step 4. Provide "music listening times" when the family gathers for no other reason than to enjoy the sound experience. Twenty-minute sessions a couple of times a week is a good start.

Step 5. Experiment, play, think musically. Provide natural family-time gatherings that involve the children, exposing them to music as part of general social experiences that include recreational as well as leisure activities. This will help your family to become increasingly sound aware.

Step 6. Regardless of the path you choose to take, stick with it. Although you may be successful in raising your child's musical interests and motivating him or her to select and learn to play musical instruments, be aware of the possibility that your child's natural abilities, or personal motivations, may in fact fall in different domains. After all, not every child can be a Mozart, a Mendelssohn, or a McCartney.

Exercise #2

The Alphabet Song: alternative style

One of the first tunes most children learn is the well-known "Alphabet Song" with its traditional melody. The purpose of the following exercise is to assist your child with mastering the alphabet.

- Select a tune with a catchy melody.
- Write out the alphabet.
- While you play the tune, sing along, replacing the actual lyrics or melody line with the letters of the alphabet.

An example of a tune that can be used for this exercise is Beethoven's Fifth Symphony. For a moment, just try and see how effortlessly the letters *A, B, C, D* fit into the first four notes of this symphony. Now try singing *E, F, G, H* along with the next four notes. As the piece continues, with the music moving faster and faster, and then slower again, try going through the whole alphabet. When you get to "Z" you may want either to go backwards, or return to "A" and start again.

A twist to this exercise that is popular among children who are introduced to it is to sing the alphabet to any number of different melodies borrowed from favorite nursery, pop, or even classical tunes.

Another way of thinking about this exercise is that the letters of the alphabet will replace the actual lyrics of the song you and your child select. As with anything else, some songs will lend themselves to this technique a little better than others. While some, you will find, will be almost impossible to fit in, others will flow quite naturally. Part of the challenge, then, is finding those melodies that you and your child will be able to convert into alphabet songs.

Another fun variation is to appoint a leader (either yourself, your partner, a friend, or one of your children) who will start out with any letter, stay on that letter over several notes, and then switch letters according to whim. The others in the group have to listen carefully, and remain constantly aware of facial expressions, gestures, voice inflections, and any other signals that may indicate when the letter switching will occur. Take turns with everyone playing the leader in round-robin style.

Sound Suggestion

Even if your child is quite comfortable with the alphabet already, it's still a good idea to have it written out in front of you as you attempt to fit it into the different melodies.

SOUND RESOURCES RECOMMENDED FOR NURTURING YOUR CHILD'S MUSICAL DEVELOPMENT

Music Menu #8
Classical music for children

Baby Needs Baroque	Various Artists
Beethoven for Babies	Various Artists
Baby Needs Mozart	Various Artists
Bach to Rock (introduction to classical music)	Rosemary Kennedy
Children's Classics	Leonard Bernstein
The Classical Child (various titles)	Ernie Mavrides
Classics for Children	Arthur Fiedler
Fiedler's Favorites for Children	Arthur Fiedler
Prokofiev: Peter & The Wolf	Leonard Bernstein

Set Your Life to Music: New-Age Classical Series	Philips Music
Strike Up the Orchestra: Child's Guide to Classical Music	Various Artists
The Classical Child at the Opera	Ernie Mavrides
The Composers' Specials	Various Artists
The Classical Kids Collection of Greatest Classics, Volumes 1 & 2	The Kids Collection
The Power of Classical Music	Victoria Rowell
Classical Kids Collection	Susan Hammond
Young Person's Guide to the Orchestra	Sir Simon Rattle

Music Menu #9
Music for teaching rhythms

This Is Rhythm	Ella Jenkins
Play Your Instruments & Make a Pretty Sound	Ella Jenkins
Adventures in Rhythm	Ella Jenkins
Counting Games and Rhythms for the Little Ones	Ella Jenkins
Rhythms, Game Songs	Ella Jenkins
Rhythms on Parade	Hap Palmer
Mother Moose Rhymes	Abrams & Anderson
	Dean Steeves

3

LISTENING

The Key to Harmony in the Home

Of all the skills children must learn as they travel along their develop-mental journeys, those of listening and communicating stand out as most fundamental. Often mistaken for "hearing and talking," the abilities to listen and communicate effectively will serve as the cor-nerstones of your child's ability to grow into a caring and respected adult. The purpose of this chapter is to introduce parents to a number of creative ways through which music and sound can be used to increase their children's listening and communication skills.

During the first four years of her life, Brittney was essentially raised by her grandmother. With a new baby, car, mortgage, and school loans to pay back, the only way we could stay above water at the time was for both Mark and I to work full-time jobs. Unfortunately, although Brittney's granny was a wonderful influence in many ways, her style of communication—and one that Brittney quickly incorporated as her own—consisted primar-ily of "interruption." Because of Granny's constant hampering with phrases like, "I know what you're going to say," "Yeah, but," and "Yes, I know…" it was basically impossible to have a conver-sation with her, and, eventually, with Brittney as well. By the time we were able to settle into our new lives and begin spending more quality time with her, Brittney had picked up so many bad habits that it took us years to undo the damage and teach her proper ways of listening and communicating.

—Paige, twenty-eight, business consultant

As parents prepare their children for a world of hastened communi-cation, one of the most nurturing gifts they can share is that of active, attentive listening. The following suggestions are given as general reminders that, when it comes to meeting the challenges posed by our brisk and bustling world, listening is the key to the kingdom of communication.

LISTENING RULES FOR EVERYBODY

Don't be a mind reader or guesser. Don't try to guess, or think that you know what the other person is going to say. Don't try to guess what they *might* say. No one likes to be interrupted.

Focus. Listen to what the person is saying, not to thoughts going on in your own head.

No rewind, and no replay. Talking with someone in person is not like watching a video or playing a CD. You will not be able to rewind and replay what they just said.

It's now or never. A lot of times you only get one chance to hear what someone is saying. It might be the rules to a game, or a fire drill announcement at school telling you which way to exit, as when an ice cream truck drives past your home playing those summoning tunes— if you don't hear it, you're out of luck!

Wait your turn. Everyone appreciates politeness. If you listen to what someone is saying to you, they will be more apt to listen to you when it's your turn to talk.

Could you say that again, please? It's not always easy to hear, or understand, everything somebody else is saying. If you need someone to repeat what they just said, don't be shy, ask.

Respect others. Even if you think that what someone is saying to you is not very important, it may actually be very important to them. Listening to others makes them feel respected. If you respect others, there is a better chance that they will respect you.

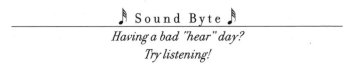

♪ Sound Byte ♪

Having a bad "hear" day?
Try listening!

LISTENING EXERCISES

As we ride the merry-go-spiral of maturation, upward and onward from infancy to adulthood, we tend to think of certain things as being automatic. Early on, we begin to separate those things we need to learn—such as math, reading, and writing, for instance—from others that will just "naturally" take care of themselves, such as breathing, digesting, or healing. Unfortunately, most of us who are blessed with the magical power of hearing often tend to include the ability to listen with the latter. Eventually, however, as many of us find out at some point during our lives, truly "good listeners" seem at times harder to find than skilled surgeons or virtuoso musicians.

> *I was about seven or eight when my mom and I were waiting for a local shuttle at the train stop and I noticed two men standing across from each other, watching each other make signals with their hands. At first I thought they were mimes, but then I asked Mom if they were dancing. She told me they were "hearing impaired," that they could not hear sound and so had to communicate with their hands and gestures. It was both the saddest and the most impressive thing I had ever seen. It was so important for these two men to communicate that they had actually learned to speak and listen with their eyes and hands. Then I noticed how many sounds were happening all around us, and realized they couldn't hear any of them. It was an awakening for me. The first time I really understood what a miraculous gift it is to be able to hear.*
>
> —Jason, twenty-two, college student

By focusing on music and sound, parents can increase their children's interest in music and at the same time enhance their overall sound awareness. The following exercises are designed to introduce parents to ways through which sound and music may be used to help fine-tune their children's skills in listening and self-expression.

FIRST AND SECOND GRADERS

The listening report. Choose a particular song for your daughter, preferably one she hasn't heard before, and ask her to come back and tell you what the song was all about. Or ask her to listen to a storybook tale on tape and then tell you in her own words what it was about.

The good and the bad. Have your daughter tell you three *bad* things that can happen when people *don't* listen. Then have her tell you three *good* things that can happen when they *do* listen.

Increasing sound awareness. Each day, ask your daughter to tell you about one new sound she heard. At first, it is very helpful if you do this together; you can point out the many different sounds we take for granted—the tone or accent of someone's voice, the general sound of traffic, or how some trucks are louder than others. It could be something as obvious as the washing machine going, or the air conditioner cutting on and off. Or it could be as subtle as birds singing or her tummy growling. If she can just come up with one, that's a good start, but listening for more new sounds will help her to remain sound aware for longer periods of time.

THIRD AND FOURTH GRADERS

Listening the "write" way. Have your son write a short report, fifty words or so, about why listening is important. After he has written the report and discussed it with you, you can then ask him to try to summarize it in one sentence.

Suggest he write a report discussing what sounds he would miss most if he couldn't hear. Or have him list his five favorite sounds, and his five least favorite sounds.

Increasing sound awareness. Each day, ask your son to tell you at least two new sounds that caught his attention during the course of the day.

Tuning in. Select a song that has very minimal instrumentation, so you can hear each instrument clearly. Have your son listen to the music and focus on one instrument at a time. Suggest that he try to follow that same instrument—for instance, a piano—throughout the entire song. Tell him that his mind will wander off to other instruments and that, when this happens, he should simply recognize this and return to listening to the chosen instrument. You can then play the song again and have him focus on a second instrument—say, a bass guitar—and then a third—perhaps a drum—each time he listens to the song.

FIFTH AND SIXTH GRADERS

Commercial music. Have your daughter watch and listen to a television commercial with a music soundtrack. Ask her to think about how the lyrics in the music are being used to help sell the product.

Increasing sound awareness. Each day, ask your daughter to tell you at least three new sounds that got her attention during the course of the day.

The "write stuff." Have your daughter write a one-hundred-word report about why listening is important. After she has written the report, you can then have her try to summarize it in one sentence.

Three Deaf Mice. Ask your daughter to think of three instances when not listening to someone could prove disastrous. Then ask her to think of three situations when listening attentively could prove very rewarding.

Empathic listening. When your daughter comes home from school, ask her to recall something someone said during the course of the day that had special meaning for her. It may be something simple, a casual greeting that made her feel acknowledged; or something negative, a comment that hurt her feelings; or something very special, maybe a commendation from a teacher or coach. As you listen empathically to her thoughts, tune in to the emotions underlying the words. Is she asking for advice, support or encouragement, or merely sharing some general observations? Using your best judgment, respond to her needs.

SEVENTH AND EIGHTH GRADERS

Interpreting messages. Ask your son to choose three popular songs from among his favorites: one that delivers a clear message, another that has hidden or double meanings, and a third that has confusing lyrics, or which makes little or no sense. Have him discuss his interpretation of each song's lyrical content, and to imagine ways in which the artists might have conveyed the song's messages a little differently.

Increasing vocabulary. Have your son go through a dictionary and select three words he's never heard before, based on the uniqueness of their sounds alone. Have him give an interpretation of what it is about these words that makes them appealing to him.

Hearing the big picture. Over a period of a week or so, have your son listen to at least eight to ten minutes of different types of music (rock, jazz, country, classical, New Age), choosing a particular music genre each night. Ask him to take notes while he listens, and, at the end of the week, have him verbally report which songs he liked or did not like, and what elements in the music (lyrics, instrumentation, harmony, melody) made some genres more appealing to him than others.

Bridging generation gaps. Choose three popular songs from among your pre-teen favorites. Then have your son select three favorites from his current collection. Have him listen to all six tunes and offer an interpretation of how the overall sounds between the two musical eras are similar, and how they are different. How do they echo, or reflect, different aspects of each time period? Some examples may be how the songs reflect the different tempos of their respective eras (current songs are typically faster); different sounds (modern songs generally have fuller and "cleaner" instrumentation); or different lyrical tones or messages (older songs tend to be less direct or obvious in content).

Food for the Ears

For younger children:
Once in a while, take a "sound day."
Accompany your young child on a sound hunt.

For older children:
Encourage your older child to go on a sound hunt,
either alone or with a friend,
and bring back the "sound loot."
(see chapter 9, Sound Hunting: Sound Safari)

Following are sound resources recommended for nurturing your child's listening, attention, focusing, and mental abilities.

Music Menu #10
Story audio books

Toddlers to preschoolers:

Baby's Story Time	Arlo Guthrie
Birds	Marie Aubinais
	and Jean-Francois Martin
Do the Angels Watch Close By?	Mary Joslin and Danuta Mayer
Fun Is a Feeling	Chara M. Curtis
Hey, Little Ant	Phillip & Hannah Hoose
It's Raining Whisper	Byrna Notrog
The Playground	Debbie Bailey
The Story of the Root-Children	Sibylle von Olfers
The Little Soul and the Sun	Neale Donald Walsch
The Mole's Daughter	Julia Gukova
Over the Moon: An Adoption Tale	Karen Katz
Sky Castle	Sandra Hanken
Bump in the Night	Jim Cummings
The Teddy Bears' Picnic	Jerry Garcia
	and David Grisman

Preschoolers to school age:

Shelley Duvall Bedtime Stories Series	Multiple Titles
Cinderella and Other Favorite Children's Stories	Storybook Classics
Grimm's Fairy Tales: Six Favorite Children's Stories	Storybook Classics
Gulliver's Travels and Other Favorite Children's Stories	Storybook Classics
Hans Christian Andersen: Six Children's Classics	Storybook Classics
Jack and the Beanstalk and Other Favorite Stories	Storybook Classics
Storytime!	Arlo Guthrie
Weezie and The Moon Pies	Bill Harley
Spiders in the Hairdo: Modern Urban Legends	David Holt and Bill Mooney
Why the Dog Chases the Cat	David Holt and Bill Mooney
Various Titles	Jim Weiss
The Lion King: Far from the Pride Lands	Disney Read-Along
The Story and Songs from the Wizard of Oz	Various Artists
In Search of the Mighty Reptar: Songs and Stories	Rugrats
Thumbelina	Audio Book Company
Animals Make You Feel Better	John Sutton
Caribou Girl	Claire Rudolf Murphy
The Castle of Birds	Polly Lawson
Coppèlia	Margot Fonteyn
Days of the Knights: A Tale of Castles and Battles	Christopher Maynard
Hanuman	Erik Jendresen and Joshua M. Greene
The Missing Piece	Jennifer Gould
My Name is Georgia: A Portrait (Georgia O'Keefe)	Silver Whistle
No Mirrors in My Nana's House (with music CD)	Ysaye M. Barnwell
The Rose's Smile: Farizad of the Arabian Nights	David Kherdian
The Secret of Old Zeb	Carmen Agra Deedy
Arthur's TV Trouble	Marc Brown
Arthur Writes a Story	Marc Brown

Madeline's Rescue	Ludwig Bemelmans
Star Wars Episode I: The Phantom Menace	John Williams
Wizard of Oz	Art Carney
Dukas: Sorcerer's Apprentice (Favorite French Spectaculars)	Leonard Bernstein
Little Proto's T-Rex Adventure: A Musical Dinosaur Story	Odds Bodkin
Arthur's Treasure Hunt	Marc Brown

TUNING IN TO LEARNING STYLES

Different people have different ways of gathering, learning, and remembering information. Although most of us learn from things we hear (auditory), see (visual), and do (kinesthetic), many of us have a particular, personal learning style with which we feel most comfortable and tend to be most proficient. Some of us may discover, for instance, that we are much better at remembering certain things when they are presented in written form. On the other hand, we may come to understand that a younger brother or older sister needs to physically apply an activity before he or she is truly able to grasp and retain the information for future use.

In essence, a "preferred" learning style is similar to being right-handed vs. left-handed, or right-brained vs. left-brained, with no one learning style being "better" or "worse" than another. When parents and their children understand that their individual learning styles are simply natural, inborn ways of perceiving the world, or preferences for certain activities, they can learn how to accept and maximize these innate abilities.

Throughout my years of practice as both clinician and consultant, I have worked with many children who exhibited an inclination toward one particular learning style over another. Proficient and highly accomplished in a number of areas, many of these children continued to feel frustrated by their inability to "tune in" to information in the same manner as a sibling or peer. Likewise, well-meaning parents, struggling to help their child through techniques that they found personally helpful in the past, find themselves at a loss when faced with a child who has a learning style different from their own, or from their other children's.

Tuning in to your children's primary learning styles is essential to helping them maximize their capabilities. It also saves time and energy otherwise spent on the well-meaning but futile effort of trying to force ways of learning that lie outside your children's natural inclinations. By becoming aware of their children's primary learning styles, parents can focus on their strengths, while also drawing from various techniques to help them compensate for their weaknesses.

The following vignettes illustrate some practical ways in which music and sound can be used effectively to accentuate each learning style.

Tyler: auditory learner. Auditory learners acquire information most easily through listening, or by *hearing* things explained to them. Although tested in the above-average range of intellectual ability, ten-year-old Tyler was unable to achieve better than average grades in a number of his classes. Attempts by his parents, both visual learners, to assist him with a number of visually oriented techniques that had worked well for them proved futile. After an exploration of Tyler's learning style found him to be primarily an auditory learner, his parents began to focus on ways in which his superior listening skills could be emphasized.

The following techniques were used:

· *Read and highlight.* Rather than simply reading his lesson plans in the evening, Tyler began using a highlighter on important points.
· *Summarize and record.* After completing each section, Tyler summarized the important concepts and read them into a tape recorder. Reading the information out loud led to putting the ideas into his own words, helping Tyler to further integrate the material.
· *Play back and listen.* When it came time to prepare for a test, rather than reviewing the written materials, Tyler rewound the tapes and played back the summaries he had compiled. After a couple of trial-and-error attempts at refining this new approach, Tyler's grades improved significantly.

In using the above techniques, it is a good idea for parents to pay particular attention to carefully labeling the tapes and using different tapes for different classes or subject areas. At the end of the school term, once that information has been integrated and used for the exam period, the tape can then be erased and used for a future class.

Briana: kinesthetic learner. Kinesthetic learners acquire information most easily through *doing* things—actively involving themselves in hands-on activities. Eight-year-old Briana was a "doer." She liked being physically involved in projects and active games, and found it difficult to communicate without animated gestures. Although she liked going to school and learning new things, she found it hard to sit still and concentrate. After attempts at having her learn her school material in conventional ways failed, her parents developed a plan through which her active learning style could be used to her advantage.

The following techniques were used:

- *Active involvement.* Having identified her as a kinesthetic learner, Briana's parents became more involved in helping her find ways to approach her studies through active, physical activities.
- *Do the right thing.* To help her with spelling, Briana's mom engaged her in nightly spelling bees. The process of sounding out words and letters helped Briana improve her pronunciation, and her vocabulary grew steadily. Math was tackled by using tangible objects she could arrange and manipulate. Learning about money, for instance, was done with coins and dollar bills, as Briana played bank teller or store clerk.
- *Talk it out.* For her other classes, Briana was encouraged to take time each night to discuss with her parents what she had learned, done, seen, and talked about during her school day. This helped her to review and later recall much more information than she had been able to understand through the more customary reading and listening approaches.

Dylan: visual learner. Visual learners have a preference for, or ease with, acquiring information through reading, or by *seeing* things taking place. Described as "quiet" and "very organized," eleven-year-old Dylan had trouble with listening and with expressing his thoughts and feelings. A visual learner, he had a keen ability to plan and arrange things in writing, but found it hard to follow through. His goals and ideas seldom made it out of the written stage and into the real world.

Drawing on his strengths, Dylan's parents pursued the following path:

- *Sharpen listening skills.* Dylan's parents had him listen to two or three popular songs (sometimes chosen by him, other times by his parents) every school night and try to write down as many lyrics as he could make out as he listened. Although he was given the option of rewinding the tape or backtracking the CD and replaying different choruses as he wished, a time limit of thirty minutes was set.
- *Engage thinking, speaking, and doing.* After he listened to the selections, Dylan would spend ten to fifteen minutes discussing with his mom or dad what the songs' primary messages were, and sharing his opinion on the story lines as deduced from the lyrics.
- *Activate feelings.* Dylan then related how he *felt* about the songs, and what he did or did not like about them.

At first Dylan found it hard to follow this exercise. But before long he began to feel more comfortable with the approach and more proficient with the techniques. Although talking about the music for even five minutes was awkward for him during the first few days, by the end of the second week Dylan's interest in the music and this process increased. His discussions with his parents extended well past the allotted time. His interest in listening to different types of music, and his ability to relate his feelings about the songs and their messages, expanded steadily.

Parents who wish to try this technique may want to decide beforehand if there are time limits that they should set, and later adhere to. As a rule, ten to fifteen minutes for listening and another ten to fifteen for discussion are good starting points.

SOUND RESOURCES RECOMMENDED FOR NURTURING YOUR CHILD'S LEARNING SKILLS

Music Menu #11
Music for general education

Disney's Pooh Learning Series (various titles)	Disney
The Mozart Effect: Tune Up Your Mind	Don Campbell
Music to Stimulate Your Baby's Brain	Baby Mozart
Beethoven for Babies: Brain Training for Little Ones	Set Your Life to Music Series
Changing Channels	Cathy Fink and Marcy Marxer
Schoolhouse Rock	Various Titles
Educational audiocassette tapes from Kimbo Educational	Various Titles
Educational audiocassette tapes from Dr. Maggie	Dr. Margaret Allen
Thinking Music Series: Sound frequencies designed to improve health, learning and thinking abilities	Applied Music & Sound

Music Menu #12
Music for learning math

123 (board book and cassette)	Sesame Street
Addition	The Fun-Damentals
Bethie's Really Silly Songs About Numbers	Bethie
Born to Add	Sesame Street
Counting Games and Rhythms for the Little Ones	Ella Jenkins
It's Time for Counting	Barney
Multiplication	The Fun-Damentals
Number Hunt with Pooh	Disney
Numbers	Sesame Street
Rap Addition	Rock 'N Learn
Rap Subtraction	Rock 'N Learn
Various Rock Titles (multiplication, subtraction, addition, division)	Rock 'N Learn
Various Country Titles (multiplication, addition, subtraction)	Rock 'N Learn

Music Menu #13
Music about historical characters

American Heroes	Jonathan Sprout
Numerous historical characters from	
American Tall Tales and Legends	Various Artists
Sing It Loud	Various Artists
This Land Is Your Land	Woody Guthrie

4

SOUND RELAXATION

Calming Your Children

Many years ago a wise physician shared with me that, in his opinion, the most important thing in the world is "peace of mind." Having worked with literally thousands of families over the years, however, it is very clear that—for parents—a calm, quiet, and peaceful child is a prerequisite for their own peaceful existence.

Having set the "sound stage" for relaxation during your child's infancy, the "seeds to soothing" will have been planted, and your growing child will be better prepared to handle anxieties and stresses. As your children mature into toddlers, preschoolers, and beyond, a lot of the basic principles you practiced during their infancy will continue to influence, and reinforce, relaxing environments and peaceful states of mind. By taking deep breaths before reacting, using moderate voice levels, communicating positively, and generally spreading "good vibrations," you will have helped to convey these skills to your child. By the time children start school, parents can begin to teach them more formal ways of relaxation, as well as more conscious ways of listening to, and handling, life's stresses and frustrations.

After a couple of years of relative normalcy, Erik, at about two and a half, began to "climb the walls." Our pediatrician told us his behaviors were normal and he would outgrow them, but at four years he was still just as hyper and unable to relax. We had him evaluated, and the doctors told us he was "normal," but just "very enthusiastic, energetic and hypersensitive," which was a relief, because we didn't know how we would have handled it if they had suggested medication. We tried a number of different things to get him to relax—exercise, games, reading stories, massage, and even music that was supposed to be relaxing, but nothing really took for very long.

One day he was playing noisily in the living room and we were playing this CD, "Inner Rhythms" by Randy Crafton, in the background. When the sixth selection, "Rag Africa"—which is a very enchanting blend of melodic percussion—came on, there was suddenly this big silence in the living room. We looked in to see if everything was all right and found Erik just sitting there, playing very quietly. As soon as the tune was over, he walked up to the stereo and hit the repeat button—something we didn't know he knew to do—so he could hear that same selection again. From that moment on, whenever we felt he needed to relax, we played that song and it always did the trick.

Soon after that, we went to a music store and asked the clerk if he could suggest other titles that were in the same genre or that featured similar melodic percussion instruments. He did, and it was as if we had struck gold! Those sounds had such an effect on Erik that a few weeks later we went to a specialty store and bought him some udu, kim-kim, and tongue drums. Now, whenever he's stressed, he pulls out those drums and plays them for twenty or thirty minutes. Sometimes he plays along with one of his CDs, other times he plays them alone, and still other times he simply listens to the CDs. Either way, those vibrations seem to be exactly what he needs to stay in tune.

—Erika, thirty-six-year-old mother and homemaker

In general, music and other soothing sounds can help to lessen anxiety and reduce stress by:

· Decreasing stress-related hormones.
· Diverting our attention from fears, worries, tension and other day-to-day concerns.
· Activating natural endorphins.
· Enhancing relaxation.
· Providing "mini mental vacations" that can even take our minds away from physical pain for a period of time.
· Clearing our minds and helping us to focus more attentively.
· Inspiring us, which helps us to look at our options and possibilities more optimistically.

- Physiologically altering body chemistry, resulting in lower blood pressure and slower respiration, heartbeat, pulse rate, and brain-wave activity.
- Promoting social interaction and expression of feelings, which encourages us to discuss and often work through our needs, hopes, fears, and concerns.
- Calming and synchronizing our internal rhythms.
- Lifting depressed moods and dispelling anger.
- Inhibiting negative, nagging thoughts and feelings.
- Mobilizing our "internal resources," stimulating us to be more "proactive."
- Helping us to gain some control over our environments.
- Blocking out external noises that tend to throw us "off-kilter."
- Aiding our bodies' immune systems, helping us to function more effectively.

(See "Music-Related Research Journals and Publications," in Appendix B, for journals including articles that consistently support and update findings in each of the above areas.)

The following segments are meant as general reminders that parents can keep in mind when searching for ways to calm their young children.

♪ Sound Byte ♪

Quiet and noise are incompatible.
If you have one you can't have the other.

MUSIC AS A SOUND SOLUTION: RELAXING INFANTS

They're picking up good vibrations. From the moment of birth, recent research shows, infants experience a number of basic emotions, such as joy and fear. If you've had a particularly stressful day at work, or a disquieting event at home, take a few moments to unwind and dispel your anxieties before approaching your infant or child. Keep in mind that your infant will "understand" (i.e., sense and react to) "vibrations" much earlier than he or she will understand words.

Nursing and a'rocking. When nursing, the calmer the mother is, the better her infant will be able to relax. A few minutes of bonding and swaying in a rocking chair, coupled with soothing background music, helps to relax both mother and child.

"Rock Steady." When rocking, or trying to calm your infant, practice deep, restful breathing. This will help to slow down your heartbeat and allow your baby to synchronize with your rhythms and relax accordingly. Soothing music with a steady pulse, such as largo movements from Baroque compositions, is very effective in helping to set a steady, calming tempo.

Slow dance. If your child is anxious, try gentle, rhythmic slow dancing to soothing tunes. Hold her close and sing or hum quietly along with the music. Your vibrations will contribute a sense of comfort and safety.

Sound Suggestion

Too much motion (fast, jittery movements, or incessant jostling) is usually a sign of frustration, anxiety, or desperation on the parent's part and should be avoided, as it will prove counterproductive or even harmful. If you feel stressed, anxious, or exasperated, take a few moments to calm yourself and become centered before attempting to calm your child. (See chapter 12, "Taking Care of Yourself: The Ultimate Investment.") If your infant continues to cry despite your attempts to soothe him, you should explore the underlying reason(s) with your pediatrician.

Hug. When hugging your child, breathe deeply, slowly, and rhythmically. Think of your two bodies merging as one. Murmur loving words and positive affirmations ("We are calm," "I love you"), or sing a soothing lullaby. Think of your hug as a loving circle, flowing within and between the two of you, cycling soothing feelings and vibrations.

Be cool. In stressful situations, take a deep breath, center yourself, and try your best to set a relaxed tone. Speak at a moderate volume. Your child will pick up on your vibrational cues and react accordingly.

Particularly when faced with a crisis, it is always best to approach the situation calmly, rather than giving in to the anxiety of the moment.

The rhythm's gonna get ya! Again, infants respond very well to rhythmic movements. Baby slings, Guatemalan "Maya wraps," and Mexican rebozos help to free your hands so that your baby can experience the rhythms of laundering, sweeping, dusting, vacuuming, or yard work. At the same time, they allow you to maintain physical contact with your baby.

Use all five (common) senses. When your infant is upset, startled, or crying uncontrollably, try the following three-step sound approach to calming him down:

Step 1. Turn on some soft, soothing music that will play for at least twenty to thirty minutes, but longer if possible. Suggestions include lullabies, soft classical or Baroque music, music-box tunes, or—for newborns—heartbeat sounds (see below).

Step 2. Look directly into your infant's eyes to communicate that you are there and his world is safe. Try slow dancing, rhythmic rocking, or another swaying movement, dictated by the music, that will help to "entrain" your child's vibrations down to a more relaxed state. (See "Musical Entrainment" at the end of this chapter.)

Step 3. Communicate soothing vibrations by speaking softly or singing or humming along with the tune. The feel and smell of your closeness will serve as additional comfort cues while offering a familiar sanctuary.

In most cases, your infant will eventually entrain to the soothing, comfortable tempos set by this multisensory approach. Once the child is relaxed, the soothing music that has helped to set the calming background will continue to serve as a peaceful anchor in maintaining a tranquil, sound environment.

"Baby, Baby, Can't You Hear My Heartbeat?" For newborns, as for everyone else, change takes some getting used to. Numerous studies conducted over the years have shown that the sound of a steady heartbeat, which essentially echoes the in-utero sound-feel experience, is most relaxing for newborns. Some very soothing heartbeat sounds can be obtained via sound-generator machines or recordings designed to simulate various natural sounds.

Use plenty of sound screen. From early on in your baby's life, you may want to start the habit of lulling your child to sleep by reading positive, happy stories in a peaceful and affirming voice. Once your child is tucked in and asleep, a sound screen—whether soft background music, drones,* "white noise,"** or nature sounds—will help to keep out intrusive, potentially startling noises, and help to ensure that your baby has a good night's rest.

RELAXING TODDLERS AND PRESCHOOLERS

Deep breathing. The simplest, most basic and effective way of relaxing oneself is through "deep breathing." This is also known as "belly" or "diaphragmatic" breathing. Parents are encouraged to introduce the process of deep breathing to their children by practicing the following exercise together:

- Lie down in a soft, warm, comfortable space. Place both of your thumbs on your belly button so that your hands and fingers rest gently over your abdomen, and have your child imitate you.
- Take in several deep breaths, consciously "aiming" the breath down into your belly.
- Ask your child to visualize or imagine the breath flowing into the nose and mouth, moving down through the body and deep into the belly, as if inflating a balloon.

---

*"Drones" are continuous, meditative sounds that can help to ground the body and relax the mind. Some natural examples are ocean waves, continuous rain, waterfalls and running water. Music-related drones are produced by instruments such as tambouras, bagpipes or harmoniums, and are typically associated with Indian or Scottish music. The sound of running water in particular has been found to be quite effective in soothing infants.

**"White noise" is a form of a drone usually identified with continuous "hushing" tones such as those provided by fans, air conditioning units, or sound screens that simulate soothing sounds.

- Feel the breath first filling up the belly and causing your hands to rise along with the abdomen.
- *After* the belly is filled, the breath will then begin to fill up the chest and lungs, *from the belly up*. (Practicing this part in front of a mirror first is sometimes helpful.)
- Once you master the above steps, try holding your breath for a count of three, then letting it out *s-l-o-w-l-y*. Rather than pushing or forcing the breath out, think of yourself as *allowing* the air to *flow* out, slowly and consciously. As the breath leaves your body, focus on the feelings of calm and relaxation that this process generates.

All aboard! A breathing analogy. In releasing your breath, the following analogy may be helpful. Remind your child that if you enter a bus, train or airplane first, and sit in the back, the people who enter *last* will exit *first* (drawing a simple diagram may be useful). Likewise, the breath that entered your body *first* went into your belly, and that will be the breath that will have to patiently wait to exit the body *last*. This simple analogy can serve as a reminder that breathing out is much like letting the air out of a balloon, or pouring water out of a flask. Having filled up from bottom to top, it will now need to exit from top to bottom. This exercise has the added benefit of teaching patience.

Encourage your child to try this exercise when she is upset. This process can also help your child fall asleep.

Following are a number of exercises that parents can consider when planning and creating sound, relaxing environments for their growing children. For each of the exercises, be sure to first set aside a comfortable, warm, quiet spot in your home where your child—and you, if you're doing it together—will not be disturbed for a period of at least fifteen to twenty minutes.

With each exercise, as with anything else that is new or different, keep in mind that your child may have problems accepting or adjusting to these techniques and suggestions. Remember these principles: first, the earlier you start practicing these techniques with your children, the more they will accept them as "normal" things that families do; and second, with support and regular practice, your children will become better at these techniques and at accepting them as part of their regular lives.

Exercise #1
Musical puffins

Age: toddlers and older

Step 1. Select one of your daughter's favorite soft, gentle tunes. It can be lyrical or instrumental.

Step 2. Before the music begins to play, take a couple of minutes to either suggest to your daughter that she begin taking deep breaths as described above, or to model the deep breathing process for her.

Step 3. After a few deep breaths, begin playing the music. While it plays, suggest to your daughter that she "breathe and puff" along with the song.

For example, rather than singing or humming along with the song's melody or lyrics, she should breathe naturally—as she would for singing, whistling, or humming—but replace the singing or humming with "musical puffs," imitating the tune's melody with short but sustained and controlled exhalations. In other words, as she is "puffing" the song, she would be taking some short and some moderate breaths—as one would for singing, humming, or whistling—and then releasing the "puff-breaths" as she would words.

Some traditional children's tunes that you may try with your child, because of their slow, flowing rhythm and tempos, could include:

Oh, Dear! What Can the Matter Be?
Home On the Range
Seeing Nellie Home
Frere Jacques

A second option, depending on how proficient or musically sophisticated she may be, would be for her to try selecting and imitating one particular instrument (bass guitar, drum beat, piano, flute) throughout the song.

The processes of concentrating on the tune, focusing breathing, and imitating the melody line will help to take her mind off her present concerns. In addition, adjusting her breathing to the soothing tempo of the music will eventually help her to entrain herself down to a calm and more relaxed mood.

(Entrainment, or "musical entrainment," in this context, can be described as a process through which we slowly orient our minds or bodies in a desirable direction. An anxious person, for example, would entrain down to a calmer, more controlled state. For a detailed introduction to "Musical Entrainment," again, please see end of this chapter.)

Exercise #2
Thought stopping: "Stop! Goes the Weasel"

Age: toddlers and older

A song that I have found to be effective as a thought-stopping tool is the traditional "Pop! Goes the Weasel." The trick is that whenever your child gets to the word "Pop!" he would replace that word with "Stop!"

Step 1. If your child is being bothered by intrusive, nagging or negative thoughts, suggest that he begin singing this song to himself. If he is in public at the time, such as at school or a mall, and cannot sing it out loud, suggest that he "sing it in his mind."

Step 2. Suggest that bothersome thoughts are sort of like "little weasels" that get inside our heads and run around giving us many silly ideas, making it hard for us to think clearly. Suggest also that we have the ability to exercise complete control over them.

Step 3. Changing the lyric to "Stop! Goes the Weasel" reminds him that he is able to make the thoughts stop so that he can then begin to feel more relaxed and think more clearly and positively.

Exercise #3
Thought stopping: tune it out!

Age: toddlers and older

A second option for helping your child block out and eliminate nagging or negative thoughts is to suggest that, as the thoughts begin to intrude, she mentally tell herself "Stop!" and then immediately begin focusing on a positive, happy song with a catchy refrain.

Some examples of traditional children's songs would be:

Did You Ever See a Lassie?
I'm a Little Teapot
Rub-a-Dub-Dub
The Hokey Pokey
A Tisket, A Tasket

Exercise #4
Drumming tension away: entrainment

Age: preschoolers and older

This exercise works particularly well for dealing with bouts of anger or anxiety.

Step 1. Help your son select one of his favorite up-tempo tunes, one that has a fairly strong (but not overpowering), steady beat. In essence, you are beginning the process by playing a tune with a tempo that closely resembles or "echoes" his current anxious or angry state.

Step 2. He may choose to stand or lie down. As the song plays, have your son inhale as he uses his fingers to gently "drum" on his chest to the beat of the music. Once he has filled his lungs and belly with air, have him stop the drumming and hold his breath for a few beats (or seconds).

After holding his breath for a comfortable period of time (say, five or six seconds), he can then begin to exhale as he resumes the gentle drumming. If he continues to feel tense after the song is done, either play it again or try a different tune that may more closely match his mood state.

Step 3. As he begins to feel more relaxed, and his anger or anxiety starts to diminish, you will then want to play increasingly slower, gentler numbers as he repeats the exercise. With slower tempo songs, suggest that he mimic the music's changing rhythms by slowing down his drumming and breathing efforts.

Exercise #5
Humming: for general, daily relaxation

Age: preschoolers and older

♪ Sound Byte ♪
───
Think of daily relaxation times as equal to other daily routines, ranking somewhere between bathtime and piano practice.

Step 1. Select a number of peaceful, serene musical selections. If you have one or two selections that can support a relaxing mood for a sustained period of time, say, fifteen to twenty minutes or longer, those tunes may be simpler and more practical to use.

If you select different numbers, make sure you program them—as on a disc player—so that they play in the right order and for the length of time you feel is right for your child's age and temperament. The length of time a child is able to relax, regardless of age, will increase with regular practice.

Step 2. Have your child lie down in her preferred, comfortable spot. Dim the lights to provide a soothing, pleasant environment. Suggest that, as the music plays, she close her eyes, focus on the melody, and *softly* hum along with the tunes.

At first your child may have difficulty adjusting to this new routine. With practice, again, she will get better at it.

Step 3. Once she becomes more comfortable with the routine, and with selecting her favorite calming tunes, you may notice that her humming has become softer, and perhaps has even seemed to stop. This is often a sign that the relaxation is occurring at a deeper level, and the humming is actually going on at a deeper level within her mind.

She may even drift off and end up taking a short nap. In a sense, this is a result of her body and mind telling her that this was just what she needed at the time. In either case, allow the process to play out throughout the intended duration and then gently nudge her back to wakefulness so that she may continue with her day's events.

On the other hand, if she continues to have problems with following this routine, and instead insists that she "just can't relax," gently suggest that she simply lie there and enjoy the music for a few minutes while taking deep breaths. If nothing else, this alone will provide a certain amount of relaxation and increase her receptiveness to trying the actual exercise at a later time.

RELAXING SCHOOL-AGE CHILDREN

Most of the techniques and exercises described above for toddlers and preschoolers will work just as well with school-age children, albeit with some minor modifications. Deep breathing exercises, for instance, can be effectively used with children of all ages.

Likewise, most of the songs mentioned will also be suitable for older children. Some older children may still find the traditional songs useful, and others may prefer to select some from their more contemporary musical libraries. By following the suggestions above, parents can help their children choose songs that—depending on their needs at the time—have either slow and soothing, or upbeat and happy tempos with positive messages.

Parents may choose a number of other sound awareness approaches and techniques to help their older, school-age children reduce stress. Some of these are described below.

Exercise #1
Laughing it out

> One of the most overlooked and underestimated forms of stress reduction is laughter. Laughter is contagious. In its best forms, it is also like a waterfall; once you get it started, it's hard to stop.

Step 1. If possible, purchase a CD or tape of children's comedy skits and save it for those emotionally rainy days. Unlike many adults, children can listen to the same routines dozens of times and still find them just as funny as they did the first time.

Step 2. Give your child some time and space. As children head into their teen years, the need for private time and space becomes increasingly important. Recognize and respect their needs.

Step 3. Suggest that your child go to his room and simply listen to the CD or tape in privacy. Most times, you'll hear giggles and laughter coming from the room within a matter of minutes. If not, you can sit down with your child and delve deeper into what may be causing the stress.

Exercise #2
Dance-athon: using entrainment

This exercise is also especially useful for a child who may be feeling stressed as well as slightly "down."

Step 1. Put together a short entrainment music sequence that your daughter may use for working through a bout of stress or tension. Begin with one or two pieces of soft, slow music that may assist her with becoming initially relaxed while bonding with her "low" vibrational state. The songs: "Oh, Dear! What Can the Matter Be?" and "Swing Low, Sweet Chariot" are examples.

Food for the Ears

By becoming more sound-aware, parents can take advantage of cues from their own children and select those tunes that the children themselves would prefer when feeling down.

Step 2. Follow up these selections with songs that are moderately faster and have a positive tone, such as "London Bridge Is Falling Down," or "Ring Around the Rosie." As your child entrains to these more dynamic sounds, continue to follow the music with more up-tempo tunes such as "My Bonnie," "Here We Go Loopy Lou," or "Itsy Bitsy Spider."

Step 3. Finally, finish up the musical stack with high-energy, upbeat tunes that will help to move your daughter into a rocking-hopping dance session and help to shake away her stress and lift her depressed mood. Some suggested tunes would be "Ta-Ra-Ra-Boom-De-Ay," "Camptown Races," and "It Ain't Gonna Rain No More."

Exercise #3
It's a Family Affair: recharging your sound systems

This exercise is meant for families who can find about twenty minutes at least two or three times per week to simply sit down together, relax, and recharge their "peace boosters."

Step 1. Select a time and place where your family may all come together for about twenty minutes for the sole purpose of relaxing and "recharging your sound systems."

Step 2. Unplug all phones, turn off beepers, television sets, etc. Dim the lights and make yourselves comfortable.

Step 3. Play moderate up-tempo music as background and sit together for about fifteen to twenty minutes, during which time the family may discuss positive things that occurred during the day. As you share this information, or receive it from your children, be encouraging and supportive. The information you share does not have to be sensational, but merely honest, sincere, and of a positive slant!

Alternative stress management approaches. Although parents may decide on a particular relaxation technique to practice on a regular basis, various techniques may be chosen and used interchangeably. In either case, a number of standard, optional relaxation approaches that families may consider are suggested below. (Please refer to General Resources, in Appendix B, for stress management book suggestions.)

Progressive relaxation	*Watching a television comedy or entertaining video*
Meditation	*Singing*
Visualization	*Playing instruments*
Autogenics	*Exercise*
Listening to music	*Massage*

Music as prevention. Aside from its potential use for reducing stress through singing, dancing, playing, listening, or encouraging writing or other stress-reducing processes, music can also be used for prevention. In effect, we can choose to think of music as an alternative, daily "multivitamin supplement."

Sound Suggestions

- Start your day by listening to enriching, positive tunes. This helps to set a positive, affirming mind-set, fine-tuning our emotions as we begin our day.
- Whenever possible throughout the day, sing, hum, or whistle a favorite tune or two. These actions release endorphins and create positive vibrations that serve to "massage" and surround us.
- Take a few minutes at some point during your day (especially early in the morning) to listen to one or two uplifting songs. Allow these songs to be your "musical escorts" throughout the day's events.
- Encourage your children to finish the day by listening to soft, peaceful music as they wind down. The music can help to clear their minds, putting worrisome events in perspective. This can also help them to relax into a good night's sleep so that they may recharge their resources and welcome the morning refreshed and energized.

By listening to music on the way to or from school, during lunch, or at any other time of the day, children can regain a sense of harmony and fine-tune their vibrational balance. A couple of examples would be listening to inspirational music when feeling down, or to relaxing music when feeling stressed or anxious. Since there may not realistically be time during your children's school day for them to take time to listen to music, perhaps they can regularly participate in musical activities such as band or chorus, or take part in musical games during recess.

♪ Sound Byte ♪

A tune a day may not keep the doctor away,
but it may help to cut down on medical visits.

SOME FINAL WORDS ON RELAXATION EXERCISES

When you first introduce these exercises into your family routines, you may encounter different levels of resistance. If this occurs, simply suggest that your children "try it for a couple of minutes." If that doesn't work, you may then give them an option between the relaxation exercise or a different form of reducing their stress or anger, such as physical exercise, singing, or simply talking, and then trying the exercise for a couple of minutes.

In most cases it is recommended that the parent have a short discussion with the child to try to ascertain what the cause of the stress may be before suggesting any particular technique or exercise. In some situations, however, parents may be able to tell what may be at the root of the problem and realize that the child merely needs "permission," or an outlet, to help release his or her tension. As in all other situations, parents should use their discretion according to the child's present mind-set, mood state, age, and temperament.

And, if all else fails, take a deep breath . . . and count to ten!

Music Menu #14
Sound resources recommended for nurturing children with relaxation

Although some of the relaxation-oriented adult music will also work to soothe older children, the following tapes and CDs were designed specifically with children in mind. In general, the tunes selected for these compilations, or written for these titles, aim to be gentler and more child-friendly in production than the adult titles. Especially with younger children, parents are encouraged to choose from among titles designed for infants, toddlers, and preschoolers.

Secondly, while many children's compilations labeled "lullabies" will serve the purpose of relaxation as well, it is suggested that parents decide which titles they will use as "sleepy-time music" and keep these separate from the ones they reserve solely for general relaxation. This will make it easier for the children to associate particular titles with relaxation and others with falling asleep. Some relaxation-oriented CDs suggested for children include:

Calm Down! Soothing Music for Hyperactive Children, and The Soothing Pulse for Children	John M. Ortiz
Play Quietly Now!	John M. Ortiz
The Mozart Effect: Relax, Daydream and Draw	Compilation by Don Campbell
Little Peace & Quiet	Rick Charette
Quiet Time	Ricardo Cobo
Quiet Moments	Greg & Steve
G'night Wolfgang	Ric Louchard
Young Turlough and His Harp (story with soothing music)	Joemy Wilson
Debussy for Daydreaming: Music to Caress Your Innermost Thoughts	Boston Pops, Detroit Symphony, et al
Relax with the Classics (collection of CDs specifically designed for relaxation)	The LIND Institute
Solitudes	Nature Trails
Music Videos for Relaxation: Quiet Time: A Visit to the Ocean Quiet Time: A Visit Through Nature	

MUSICAL ENTRAINMENT: USING MUSIC TO MODIFY YOUR MOODS AND "ADJUST" YOUR VIBRATIONS

Basically, musical entrainment is a technique through which we can select and arrange a number of music selections to help change our moods in any way that we choose or need. It is a technique most pre-adolescents and teenagers (as well as adults) instinctively use, in one form or another, without being consciously aware of it.

Being a kid is hard enough without having to put up with my parents. Whenever they say something that really ticks me off, which is pretty often, I just go in my room and slam the door. I plug in my guitar, turn my amp way up, and play as loud and fast as I can so that I can't hear them. I get so mad that I feel like my head is going to explode and playing loud music is better than scream-ing. It really helps to get my anger out. After a while, the music starts sounding too loud, even for me, so I start turning it down.

*If they leave me alone long enough I eventually end up playing
some ballads or just tinkering, and then I can go back and face
the world again without making a jerk out of myself.*
                          —Austin, sixteen, high school sophomore

For an entrainment technique to work most effectively, it is best to follow three basic steps:

(a) synchronize the vibrations (to match one's mood),
(b) create a vibrational bridge (to go from the mood you want to get rid of, to the one you want), and
(c) settle into your vibrational destination (get to the mood you want or need).

Entrainment techniques can be used to help move people out of unwanted moods and into preferred ones, as from anger to peace, sad to happy, or lazy to stimulated.

The example below, however, is designed for the child who may be hyperactive or overly stimulated, and needs some help in calming down. Entrainment techniques can be helpful for children of most ages but they tend to be more effective with toddlers and older children, as well as adolescents and adults.

USING MUSICAL ENTRAINMENT TO CALM DOWN AN EXCITED OR "HYPER" CHILD

Step 1. *Matching your mood: Synchronizing the vibrations.* Parents will want to try to match (or approximate) their child's present mood to music that sounds close to how the child feels or is acting at the moment. If your daughter is feeling overly agitated, for instance, you would select music that sounds or "feels" very upbeat, or fast and raucous. In other words, music that reflects a boisterous feeling. For most people these are fast-tempo songs that urge you to get up and dance or jump around. The tunes may be instrumental or may have lyrics. Generally, parents will want to choose enough selections for the music to last approximately twelve to fifteen minutes. In some instances, however, more time, say fifteen to twenty minutes, may be needed to help your child to "entrain" to the music before she can move down from her excitable state.

Step 2. *Bridging the gap: Creating a vibrational bridge.* The parent, with or without the child's input and assistance, chooses a number of music selections (again, to last around twelve to fifteen minutes) that are mid-tempo, or moderately more soothing. Although these would still be active tunes, they would have a beat or "feel" that would motivate one to move around at a somewhat calmer, more moderate pace, rather than jumping and dancing around.

Step 3. *Calming down: Settling into your vibrational destination.* Finally, you will want to select twelve to fifteen minutes of music that "feels" or sounds the way you would like your child to feel by the end of the exercise. For musical entrainment to guide children from feeling rather excitable and disorderly, to more calm and relaxed, for instance, you would ordinarily want to conclude the music sequence by playing relaxed, tranquil music that would help to "sedate" your child down to a more serene and peaceful mood state. Titles I suggest in Music Menu #14 use a pulse entrainment™ technique specifically designed to calm children using this entrainment method.

CHOICES, CHOICES

Finding out Paul's musical preferences was no different than fig-uring out his favorite foods or toys. We just tried different things and, little by little, we figured it out together. It was sort of like checking out different restaurants or finding what fabrics your body is most comfortable with. You've got to enjoy the process.
—Alex, thirty-one, househusband and
greeting card designer

In most—if not all—cases, it is best to select music preferred by the person you want to help. One way to do this with children is to ask them if they can tell you some songs that *sound the way they feel at the moment.* You may also ask them if they can tell you what songs sound the way they would *like* to feel. Although the process is much more effective if they willingly participate in it, they may be unable, or at first unwilling, to cooperate. In such situations, try selecting tunes from among your child's favorites that you feel may do the trick. The type of music (children's songs, popular music, classical, New Age, jazz, country) does not matter. The important thing is to select a number of tunes that begin with music that matches your child's mood and arrange them in order so that they become increasingly calmer as the sequence moves along. By arranging the songs in this manner, one is often able to assist the child (or adult) listening to the entrainment chain in moving from the unwanted mood to a desired one. Once the tunes are selected and the order is decided, it is most practical to simply record them on a tape. This way, either you or your child will be able to replay the tape in other situations when she or he experiences similar feelings.

Sound Suggestions

- Arrange the songs in order so that you have between thirty and forty-five minutes of music, progressing from "very animated" through "moderately lively" to "tranquil and composed."
- For practical purposes you may prefer to tape-record these songs in order on a ninety-minute (forty-five minutes each side) tape. You will then be able to use the same taped entrainment sequence in future situations when your child needs a tool to help her calm down.
- As a final step, once you have recorded the musical entrainment sequence on side one, you may want to use side two to fill the tape with forty-five minutes of quiet, soothing songs. Once you guide your child through the entrainment on side one, and she has moved away from her hyperactive mood, she may then play side two, which will serve to further reinforce and maintain her feelings of comfort and well-being.

IF THAT DOESN'T WORK...

Depending on your child's particular circumstances, and her temperament, you need to decide how to best present the musical entrainment idea. Since similar situations may vary greatly from child to child, and event to event, parents can try a number of different approaches.

Option 1. If your daughter is willing to participate in the song selection, have her become actively engaged in the process. Encourage discussion about which songs in her collection sound most like she feels, and which sound as she would like to feel. Involve her in every step of the process, including thinking and talking about the songs, placing them in order, finding the tape recorder, and showing her how the songs can be recorded in sequence. Quite often, the mere process of doing the above, which gives her a sense of control, will help to get your child out of her raucous mood.

Option 2. If your child is unwilling to assist with the song search, you might ask if she would like to go to the local music store and perhaps *assist you in choosing* a new tape or CD to fit the occasion. The act of getting out of the house and into making a new purchase often stimulates people and gets their natural resources going. During the trip you can discuss the different types of music she could consider to help her to "adjust" her mood, and how *she* will be in charge of making that responsible decision.

Option 3. If the above doesn't work, you may try choosing a few selections yourself and playing parts of them for your child, again asking her to help you in deciding which may be best. This will help to reinforce her feelings of self-worth and help her to feel useful. If she is resistant or acts indifferent, simply proceed on your own; mere curiosity about what you are doing will often inspire involvement.

Regardless of the situation, respect her feelings. Listen. Provide comfort, support, and acceptance. Be sensitive to her interpretation of the situation. Asking for her assistance conveys a sense of respect and trust, while giving her a sense of control over and responsibility for her own welfare. Any process that helps to mobilize her resources will be a step in the right direction.

Music has many elements that help to trigger associations, stimulate thoughts, and activate emotions. This makes it a wonderful tool that can complement other approaches we use to help our children. Once the selections are made, for instance, the songs may be played in the background as you help your child to process her feelings and assist her in finding a "silver lining" to the situation.

5

SOUND STIMULATION

Using Music and Sound to Jump-Start Your Children

One of the most common concerns I hear from the parents in my workshops and clinical practice involves their children's lack of involvement in hands-on and physical activities. Alarming amounts of time spent playing video games, e-mailing friends and watching television have easily surpassed the large amounts of time that parents themselves used to sluggishly spend on the telephone when they were youngsters. Rather than meeting their needs for active socialization and exercise with peers by running around the yard burning calories and developing gross motor skills, children increasingly engage in isolated, sedentary activities. Although engagement in many computer-related activities will likely prove extremely useful and beneficial in our rapidly changing, computer-oriented world, the problem remains in the sense that a balance is not being met.

The fact that free time in our modern households is about as precious a commodity as water in the Sahara makes it hard for parents to find time to play active games with their children. As a result, many parents dash home from work in rush-hour traffic just in time to pick up (or meet) their children, who are then "babysat" by video games while the exhausted parents tend to dinner and immediately pressing daily responsibilities, and prepare for the next, hectic day. With increasing personal responsibilities and professional demands chipping away at precious family time, parents can use music as a tool in motivating their children to move away from their "virtual worlds," and back into actual social activities. The purpose of this chapter is to suggest a number of "musical tools" parents may consider for "jump-starting" their otherwise inactive children.

From the moment Adam and I brought Becky home from the hospital on the day after she was born, we've always played the

same music around the house that we liked when we were kids.
She must have inherited her music taste from us, because from day
one she's never been able to sit still whenever she hears uplifting
songs like Billy Joel's "Uptown Girl," or Elton John's "Crocodile
Rock." She went through a period during her toddler and kinder-
garten years when she was very much into children's tunes, but as
soon as she started school she went right back to our seventies and
eighties music. Regardless of her mood, those songs always get her
shaking and smiling.

—Marge, thirty-seven-year-old mother,
bicyclist, and school counselor

As any parent who has witnessed the hilarious, multirhythmic, puppetlike movements of young infants responding to upbeat music knows, music can be quite a stimulant. Years before children learn about caffeine, and hours after the stimulating effects of the latest herbal supplements wear out for Mom and Dad, music gets us kicking and keeps us ticking. As a stimulant, music has few—if any—rivals.

Here are ten reasons why music can serve as a safe and healthy stimulant:

(1) *It is recyclable.* One can be animated by the same song, tape, or CD *literally* thousands of times (regardless of what the music companies try to tell us, we can *still* play those old vinyl LPs!).

(2) *It is natural.* As long as played by acoustic instruments, of course.

(3) *It is (or can be) time-specific.* Selections can be consciously made to set and maintain specific tempos, depending on the pace we need at the moment.

(4) *It is programmable.* Selections can be programmed to play for specific periods of time, depending on how long we need to be invigorated by them.

(5) *It is diverse.* As we enter the new millennium, the types of music readily available are enough to satisfy, and expand, our most ambitious frontiers.

(6) *It is unprejudiced.* Music can be invigorating for all ages, races, cultures, belief systems, ethnic groups, etc.

(7) *It is endlessly optimistic.* No matter how many times one listens to a rousing, spirited song—whether lyrical or instrumental—that song's message and vibrations continue to be exactly the same.

(8) *It is refreshing.* Physiologically, music activates endorphins and vitalizes our respiration, pulse rate, heartbeat, and brain wave activity.

(9) *It is within our complete control.* Unlike other stimulants, we have complete control over when to turn our music on or off, turn the volume up or down, or switch modes at the touch of a button. (This is perhaps why it tends to be particularly irritating when someone is playing loud music, with vibrations that we do not need or want at the moment—because that music is beyond our ability to control or regulate.)

(10) *It makes a great partner.* Music is an excellent workout buddy who's always around—and never complains—*whenever* it's time for our daily exercise program.

INFANTS

Most adults are intrigued and entertained by infants merrily hopping and bopping, jiggling and wiggling to upbeat tunes and rhythmic sounds. A parent's quest for the sounds, beats, melodies, and rhythms that rouse their babies can be as exciting as the multirhythmic gyrations the babies exhibit. During these early periods of life, it is as if the infants are affirming their right to movement, surrendering to every pulse and sensation with an abandon and lack of inhibition that will likely never again be experienced so fully. Regardless of their age, the time to expose your children to upbeat, rhythmic music of varying tempos and time signatures to help broaden awareness of cross-cultural polyrhythms, exotic meters, and transworld melodies is *now*!

From the moment of birth, newborns are highly receptive to, and hungry for, all sorts of stimulation. Day one is a good time to begin introducing your child to a world of multisensory artistic and creative possibilities.

Following are a number of music-related exercises and ideas suitable for motivating and activating children.

Play stimulating music in its many guises. Musical preferences, which begin to evolve during the first few months of life, can be as diverse and colorful as our personalities. What may be particularly arousing for one child could be annoying or uninteresting to another—even within the same household. Experiment, and be sound-aware of your baby's preferences.

Rhythmic rocking. Newborn infants are very responsive to rocking, swaying and any other rhythmic movements, especially when these are accompanied by music. Hold your newborn in your arms and dance to some favorite music playing in the background. Simple, rhythmic games such as pat-a-cake, and exposure to simple, melodic sounds, will get them started on the road to musical mindfulness.

Singing. Babies love the reassurance that is conveyed through the enveloping vibrational security of a lullaby. Rather than to voice quality or lyrical precision, infants tune in to the sincerity of a parent's feel, the genuineness of the love in your voice. As you sing, hum, or whistle to your baby, detach from the ego, and focus on the uniqueness of your connection.

Dancing. Infants begin to "dance" well before they start to walk. Play music and watch your baby's rhythms activate his jiggling-bouncing responses. Once he's up and gamboling about, encourage moving to rhythmic music—it is enormously effective in getting him in touch with his natural body rhythms and the wonders of his developing muscular capabilities. This is a good time to begin to encourage the mimicking of simple rhythmic movements by assisting with hand-claps, and manipulating his feet in dancelike movements.

Musical toys. Toys with musical components can serve as excellent introductions to the world of multisensory environments. By arousing curiosity and introducing novel avenues of excitement, toys in general, and musical ones in particular, function as extremely effective physical motivators. Musical toys serve to animate many children who show little interest in regular toys.

From infancy on, the dimension of sound seems to add a touch of magic that makes an otherwise mundane toy or plush animal come to life. From rattles and ankle bells to plush singing animals, musical toys are an excellent way to introduce infants to our sound world. Providing these toys will stimulate your children into exercises that will help them develop muscle tone, gross motor skills, and coordination, while helping orient them to the surrounding environments.

When choosing from among the many excellent musical toys available for children of varying ages, pay particular attention to:

- *Safety, safety, safety.* Although many of the toys manufactured today are designed with safety in mind, it remains parents' responsibility to use every precaution when choosing toys for their children. Keeping toys with small, detachable pieces away from infants and toddlers, and sharp, jagged or fragile toys away from all children, is always a good rule of thumb. Keep battery-powered toys away from young children, as loose batteries could pose a hazard. Read labels to assure that materials are not toxic, and try to select quality toys, made by reputable manufacturers, that will not break. Also, keep electrical toys in a safe place, and make sure your children don't take them into the bathroom, swimming pool, Jacuzzi, or any other areas where water could present a risk.
- *Age relevance.* Judge a toy's appropriateness by the recommended "age-appropriate" labels, using your own judgment as to what is suitable for your child.
- *Personal magnetism.* Choose toys your infant or toddler is particularly attracted to while at a nursery or visiting at a friend's home, rather than those she sees in a crowded, highly stimulating store environment.
- *Quality.* Whenever possible, choose toys that feature clear, melodious tones.
- *Multisensory toys.* Although a lot of fine toys are available that provide a multitude of "bells and whistles," it is sometimes wise to focus on those that accentuate the one or two (e.g., visual, auditory) modalities you want your child to focus on.
- *Price.* Children soon outgrow most toys. Be prudent; expensive does not always mean quality.

TODDLERS

Children ages two to four years are typically quite egocentric and self-absorbed. By recognizing that this is a period during which children are primarily interested in their own world, and rarely engage in cooperative play *with* others, be it adults or their peers, parents can help feed their yen for sound exploration.

The toddler years, a time in which children are gaining increased control of their bodies and experiencing the joys of freedom and movement, are ideal for introducing active musical games that can involve either one or several children.

Aside from serving as a motivational tool to stimulate your toddler, music provides a number of other benefits. Used with sound awareness, music can be adapted to:

(1) Motivate children to exercise.

(2) Increase body awareness.

(3) Activate the development of gross motor skills.

(4) Improve coordination.

(5) Develop confidence and self-esteem.

(6) Act as a catalyst for imaginative improvisation.

(7) Introduce and maintain structure in organized activities.

(8) Function as a source of fun and enjoyment.

(9) Encourage social interchange.

(10) Create controlled environments where self-expression can be manifested.

Suggested music. As with infants, aside from using traditional children's tunes, parents are encouraged to expose their growing children to as many upbeat types, styles, and genres of musical forms as they feel may be properly stimulating and entertaining.

Some traditional songs that help to stimulate young children include:

Skip to My Lou	*Camptown Races*
It Ain't Gonna Rain	*Ta-Ra-Ra-Boom-De-Ay*
The Happy Wanderer	*The Hokey Pokey*
Old MacDonald	*Row, Row, Row Your Boat*

This Old Man	*Oh Susannah*
She'll Be Comin' Round the Mountain	*Take Me Out to the Ballgame*
She Wore a Yellow Ribbon	*Whistle While You Work*

(For a short description of music types and hybrids that parents may consider for augmenting their children's—and their own— sound awareness to our current musical universe, please refer to Music Menu 28, "Quick Glossary of Popular Music Styles," in Appendix A.)

PRESCHOOLERS

As they prepare for school, children begin to develop social modes of interaction and to engage in more integrated peer-related activities. Although still quite self-involved, they are more open to exploring some group activities.

Along with their growing social interests and ability to take part in communal activities, children ages four to six are more apt to partici- pate in traditional organized musical activities. In effect, all of the above benefits gained by toddlers at an elementary level are further refined throughout this age range.

Continued exposure to diverse music types and genres is rec- ommended, along with selections of traditional children's songs. For this age range, however, parents may try upping the ante in terms of the level of structure required for the musical games and activities.

Before embarking on invigorating musical journeys with your children, a few basic rules are suggested:

(1) Provide an open space, indoors or out, where the children will be safe (remove rugs they might trip on and move furniture they could bump into, as well as breakables).
(2) Set a time limit and stick to it.
(3) Although you need to have your own self-defined set of limits, rules, and boundaries well thought out before you begin, allow room for the children to freelance and be as loose and unre- stricted as possible.

Exercise #1
From Rubber Duckie to Snoop Dogg

Most children love animals, and most animals love children. A simple exercise for motivating young children involves playing various forms of music and suggesting that they dance and move around, parroting their favorite animals or insects. Some perennial favorites include dinosaurs, puppies, ducks, cats, elephants, penguins, snakes, spiders, and ants. Simple costumes and makeup go a long way toward increasing their involvement and fun.

Exercise #2
Walking in rhythm

Take fifteen to twenty minutes and suggest that your child join you in a musical walk. Before you take off, sit down and write down a number of tunes that you will sing together while you walk, or bring along a small, portable tape/CD player that you can use to play some brisk, pace-setting, sing-along tunes. Although marches are fun, any stimulating tunes, such as the ones suggested at the end of this chapter (Music Menu 16), lively popular songs, or CD compilations specifically designed for "activating your child" will do the trick.

Exercise #3
Acting out

Select a few of your child's favorite traditional tunes which contain lyrics that lend themselves to animated choreographing. Some obvious examples are songs such as "The Hokey Pokey," and "Simon Says," but, with a little creativity, parents can build up quite a backlog of "acting-out" songs to help animate their children. Tunes such as "She'll Be Comin' 'Round the Mountain" and "Row Your Boat" would fit this exercise, where the children—or a parent and child—can play the song and act out the lyrics. Numerous well-known pop songs, such as "Ghostbusters" (Ray Parker Jr.), "Let's Go Crazy" (Prince), or "Wake Me Up Before You Go Go" (Wham!) can also be used to help motivate physical activity, with participants acting out any range of impromptu to lavishly choreographed versions of the songs. (For more contemporary suggestions, see Music Menu 16 at the end of this chapter.)

Sound Suggestion

Parents are strongly encouraged to preview songs and videos before allowing their children access to them.

Exercise #4
Active goofing

An increase over the past few years in the popularity of silly or "goofy" songs gives parents a rich vein from which to select specific tunes for active fun and recreation. Borrowing tunes from contemporary performers, parents can help to motivate their children to put on "Goofy Performances," giving them permission (within a controlled context) to actively engage in showcasing the wild song lyrics and music. If a number of children are present, parents can set up friendly competitions, with the children taking turns "goofily" acting out the various characters, voices, or scenes depicted in the songs. Older CDs by artists such as Weird Al Yankovic, Ray Stevens, and Ren and Stimpy, with silly voices and parodies of well-known popular songs, continue to appeal to young children. (For more contemporary suggestions, see Music Menu 25.)

Exercise #5
Music video parodies

Many parents know how effective the highly popular music exercise videos are in getting, and keeping, adults, or children, motivated to exercise. Likewise, just as songs can be used to help motivate either planned or "off-the-cuff" active performances, video versions of popular tunes can also be taken advantage of for similar adventures. Much as described in the exercises above, parents can use music videos to help instill numerous "controlled activities" and playful movements by suggesting that the children act out their own interpretations of their favorite music videos. With a little improvising and supportive encouragement from parents, children can use a number of regular household items to safely simulate "virtual" instruments. Some of these, like "guitars" (whisk broom, tennis racket), "drums" (a couple of sticks or wooden spoons, some pillows or boxes), "synthesizers-keyboards" (end table, small step ladder, ottoman, tray cart), or "horns" (empty plastic bottles, empty paper-towel or plastic tubes) will add a fun dimension to their musical experience at little to no expense.

SCHOOL-AGE CHILDREN

School-age children are at a prime age for introduction to our universe of musical opportunities and sound possibilities. The combination of rapid mental growth, boundless energy, and increasing physical capabilities makes them excellent candidates for many exciting music-related activities.

By the time children reach this age range, many of the social, cultural, and other personal experiences accrued through their developmental journey during the first six years of life have begun to pay off. Beginning in first grade or kindergarten, children are influenced by their friends and the types of music, games, and other peer-related activities they learn at school. During this stage in their development, children are still at an age during which they are eager to learn from, and participate with, Mom and Dad.

The following exercises focus on using music as a motivating tool to inspire your children to benefit from physical workouts while bonding with you or their friends.

Exercise #1
We're all here together: exercising with your children

Exercise videos, made enormously effective by the tempo-pacing, energy-fueling rhythms of popular or programmed music, provide another rich resource that parents can use to inspire and coordinate physical activities for, or with, their children. In fact, the many types of inexpensive and versatile music exercise videos available can serve a dual purpose for parents willing to share their exercise time with their children. Prepackaged exercise videos, whether purchased or taped on your VCR for later viewing, make it possible for parents to fulfill their physical workout needs while bonding with, and role modeling for, their children. A sound suggestion is to choose those music videos that are mutually attractive to both parties.

Exercise #2
Thank you for being a friend: exercising with a friend

As stated above, this is a period during which children will increase their social activities with same or similar-age peers. Parents are encouraged to allow their children to select exercise music videos that their children can enjoy with a close friend. Generally, the true goal of this activity is to motivate your child to engage in actual physical exercise while partaking in a *controlled* and purposeful activity. As a result, it is usually best to limit the number of participating friends to one, or maybe two, who are truly interested in taking part in the program. Provide a space for the children, help them to select an appropriate exercise music video not to exceed twenty to thirty minutes in length, and loosely monitor the activity, adding encouragement and support.

Exercise #3
Yard music: exercising in fresh air

If you have a yard or an exercise area, consider supplying the indoor-outdoor area with a sound system through which you can help to encourage lively activity through stimulating music. Because children are generally much more interested in the type and volume of the music played, rather than the quality, a sound system can be something as basic as a portable "boom-box," an inexpensive radio tuned to a popular station, or simply unit speakers from a home system placed near a window and faced out toward the yard or play area.

Exercise #4
Branching out: exercising social skills

Inquire about any stimulating, social musical activities that may be available at your child's school, the local community center, or your house of worship. These organizations often provide the time, space, and resources for children to engage in safe, well-monitored activities, and to improve their social skills and self-esteem by engaging in diverse activities with other children and adults. Further, parents can take advantage of "alone time" to run errands and take care of other needs or responsibilities, freeing them to spend quality time with the children later in the evening.

Although designing structured sound activities can be fun and very beneficial, it can also be time-consuming and often impractical. When time permits, however, many parents can engage in creative ideas designed for maximizing "fun time" with their children while increasing their overall sound awareness. The following are meant as general suggestions for creating stimulating musical and sound environments for school-age children.

Music Menu #15
Music for physical fitness

The following titles are designed to provide structured exercise programs for children.

Audio:

Preschool Aerobic Fun	Georgiana Stewart
Good Morning Exercises for Kids	Georgiana Stewart
Rock 'n' Roll Fitness Fun	Georgiana Stewart

Video:

Infant Massage	Cheryl Brenman
Chicken Fat: The Youth Fitness Video	Kimbo Educational
Yoga Practice for Kids	Patricia Walden

In addition to physical fitness, well-rounded children benefit from positive challenges that stimulate them to tap into their creative muse and develop fresh, innovative ways of looking at the world and dealing with emerging situations. The following exercises are designed to promote self-exploration, and inspire children to tap into resources that will trigger independent thinking and gain awareness to diverse ways of listening to themselves and the world.

Exercise #1
Educate me

Encourage your children to teach or show you some of the new games and dances they are learning at school. Be actively interested and provide positive, encouraging feedback and support for their efforts.

Exercise #2
From "Cats" to "The Lion King"

Encourage your children to invite their friends over and put on plays, recitals and other functions that use music as a motivational force. If they need some added assistance (or supervision), you can help them in areas such as choreographing, props, and costume design.

Exercise #3
Video sensations

If you have a video camera, this is a good time to begin a second career as a producer. Encourage your children to perform for the camera to different musical soundtracks of their choosing. This will help to stimulate their creative juices and push them to extend their creative boundaries.

Exercise #4
Karaoke

School-age children are at the perfect age for Karaoke. CD and tape compilations of thousands of popular and children's tunes are available to help your child evolve from crying the blues to blues singer.

Exercise #5
Let-go your ego

As you continue to participate, or help to coordinate, your child's musical activities, remember to set your ego aside and allow your children to lead, set the tone, and select different types of music. This will further enable your children's development of healthy, positive identities.

Exercise #6
Bravo!

By this age, many musically oriented children will have made the transition from musical toys to actual musical instruments. Again, encourage them to perform their special musical numbers, lending unconditional support without expectation or judgment.

Exercise #7
Virtual virtuosos

If actual instruments are not yet in the picture, encourage a "virtual instrument" concert performance. Have your children select some of their favorite songs and put on a "virtual concert," mimicking their favorite music video artists.

Exercise #8
Keep on dancing

Although children of this age love to dance, they typically prefer to do it either in privacy—in front of a mirror—or in the guise of anonymity within a crowd of friends. Clear out some space in the den, garage, or family room, provide a reasonably adequate sound system, and allow your children—and their friends—to have regular music parties where they can progress from shedding their booties to shaking them.

The initial exposure to the musical universe that parents give to their children from day one should be continued throughout every stage of development. Although by the time their children reach adolescence their musical preferences will be fairly well entrenched, nurturing parents will have gained an insurmountable head start in planting the seeds of expanded musical sound awareness.

Encouraging your children's growing involvement in musical activities, whether for relaxation or stimulation, will help to enable their overall sound awareness, attuning them to themselves and others, as well as to their evolving sound environments. As they mature, the conscious use of music will help them develop an increased sense of activity as an exercise, integrating body awareness with refined gross and fine motor skills. While helping to improve their levels of attention and coordination, the conscious use of sound and music to complement other activities will help your children form more healthy, confident self-images by inspiring self-expression, imaginative improvisation, and a sense of rhythmic organization. By raising awareness to pace-setting in social situations, the latter will contribute to your children's ability to develop patience, or the ability to "wait one's turn" in pressure-filled situations, an invaluable asset to have when engaging in competitive activities and bonding with peers and adults.

Regardless of their age, the music your children play or listen to, the instruments they choose, the songs they sing, their inflections and intonations, their attempts at harmony and melody, their renditions and compositions, are all extensions of themselves. When they sing, play, or perform for you, they are reaching out from the core of their vibrational existence. Hear their sound and *listen*, for this is who they truly are. As you listen, always be sound aware.

HIGH ENERGY/STIMULATING

Many of the stimulating music CDs marketed for children are actually compilations of popular 50s, 60s, and 70s tunes that many parents may already have in their homes. Before purchasing these compilations, first check the song titles. Parents are also encouraged to sort through "Rock 'n' Roll Collection" sections at used CD stores, as prices there are usually about half that of new CDs.

The following titles are specifically designed to appeal to children of varying age groups.

Music Menu #16
Music for active motivation

> Although a lot of the following titles are ideal for use in conjunction with physical exercise programs such as those discussed earlier (see Music Menu 15), these, in particular, present more versatile options for rousing your children to action for no other purpose other than enjoyment itself.

Moving with Mozart	Kimbo Educational
Baby Dance: A Toddler's Jump on the Classics	Bolshoi Theatre Orchestra
Born to Add: Great Rock 'n' Roll	Sesame Street
Bounce Along with Big Bird	Sesame Street
Fingerplays and Action Chants	Tonja Evetts Weimer
Bedrock Hop	The Flintstones

Barnyard Fun	Just For Kids
Barnyard Beat	Kid Rhino
Bananaphone	Raffi
Raffi Radio	Raffi
Philharmonic Fool	Rick Scott
The Mozart Effect: Mozart in Motion	Compilation by Don Campbell
Children's Party Time: 15 Party Games and Songs	Storybook Classics
Dana's Best Sing and Play-along Tunes	Dana
Happy Feet	Fred Penner
Bumping and A-Jumping	Bananas in Pajamas
A Child's Celebration of Rock 'n' Roll	Various Original Artists
I Can Dance	Kidsongs
2BA Master: Music from the Hit TV Series Pokemon	Various Artists
Reggae for Kids Series	Various Artists
Changing Channels	Cathy Fink and Marcy Marxer
Swingin' in the Rain: Classic Swing Tunes for Kids of All Ages	Maria Muldaur
Happy Feet with a Silly Beat	Joanie Bartels
Kids in Motion	Greg and Steve
Little Hollywood	Rory
Blue Suede Sneakers: Elvis Songs for Kids!	Various Popular Artists
The Chipmunks Sing the Beatles Hits	The Chipmunks
The Parakeet Album: Songs of Jimmy Buffet	The W.O. Smith Music School Singers
Snoopy's Classiks on Toys (Beatles, classical, country or jazz music)	Snoopy
21 Really Cool Songs	The Sugar Beats
Everybody Is a Star	The Sugar Beats
Back to the Beat	The Sugar Beats
Shake Your Doodles	Allegro's Window
Fun Rock! Kooky, Crazy, Classic Rock for Kids!	Various Original Artists
Kids Wanna Rock	Mr. Al
Every One of Us	Sooz
Sing with the Animals (Animal Planet)	Various Original Artists
Beyond Pink	Barbie, Christie and Teresa
Mighty Morphin Power Rangers: The Movie	Various Original Artists

Re-Bops Jukebox! Party Songs	Re-Bops
Motor City Music for Minors	Re-Bops
Raised on Rock 'n' Roll	Re-Bops
Oldies for Kool Kiddies	Re-Bops
Circus Magic: Under the Big Top	Linda Arnold
Hippity Hop (various artists)	Linda Tillery
Playtime Favorites	Favorites Series

6

SLEEPY-TIME

From Rock-a-Bye Baby to Digitized Waterfall Sounds

Among the many factors that contribute to a happy, healthy child, a nurturing, safe home environment, unconditional love, a healthy diet, regular exercise, and a good night's sleep all rank right at the top. As they struggle to meet the increasing responsibilities posed by everyday demands, many parents' lives are further complicated as they try to adjust to their children's vacillating sleeping patterns, compounded by energy reserves that seem to kick in at just about bedtime. On the other hand, parents sometimes find that one or more of their children may actually be struggling with insomnia.

Although children vary widely in their sleeping habits, there are some general guidelines that can help parents determine whether their child is suffering from insomnia, or whether her sleeping problems fall within a common or reasonable range. A child who tends to be sleepy during the day, is irritable or fatigued, or is not functioning up to his or her potential, may not be getting enough sleep. Insomnia may involve problems in getting to sleep, staying asleep throughout the night, and/or waking up too early. A child who is *not* having these problems should, for the most part, be well rested, lively, and functioning up to par for his or her age level.

Our days would end, and begin, to the sound of Dad's voice. My brother Luis and I would climb into our bunkbeds and Dad would come in and tell us a story about "the old days." They were funny and warm and had these little morals that would somehow always help us forget any worries we may have been carrying around. He always made it safe to go to sleep. In the morning, he'd wake us up for school and then sit by our beds and tell us an inspirational anecdote, usually related to something that was going on in our lives at the time. We never figured out where he got these tales, whether he made them up, lived them,

or read them somewhere. But it didn't matter. Again, he made it
safe to face the day.

—Brandon, twenty-four, graduate student,
electrical engineering

As they mature, children will need different amounts of sleep that will decline from birth through their teens. In general, however, the following basic guidelines apply.

SOUND SLEEPING GUIDELINES

- Between ages two and eight, the amount of sleep children need decreases from about thirteen to about eleven hours per night. The amount of sleep typically required by children between the ages of ten and twelve is about ten hours, and decreases to eight to nine hours per night as children enter their teens and grow into adulthood.
- Children between the ages of two and five will commonly struggle with mild sleep disturbances. These are often described as restlessness among two- to four-year-olds, and as "bad dreams" that peak between the ages of four and six (but can persist until around age ten). If these disturbances are more than mild or temporary, the parents should consult their family doctor or a psychotherapist.
- Some common reasons for school-age children's not being able to fall asleep include noises, worrying, and restlessness.
- Standard "sleepy-time" reported by most parents is between seven and nine o'clock.
- For many—though not all—children, problems in falling asleep are a reality, not a con game, manipulative ploy, or control issue. A parent's role, therefore, is to help their children get through this transition by being supportive, attentive, and caring.

INFANTS: ROCK 'N' ROLL, THE EARLY YEARS

As most parents know, rocking is a very effective way of lulling a baby to sleep. Rocking accompanied by a soft lullaby is even more successful. Although babies seem to find comfort from the combination of the voice and vibrations coming directly from the person doing the cradling, playing soothing music or lullabies in the background while the child is being rocked is also very effective.

If noise or random sounds pose a problem, a very effective tool that helps to eliminate these disturbances is a "sound screen" or "white noise" machine. These machines can offer a very diverse range of fairly realistic-sounding, soothing nature sounds. Some of these can also be set with a timer so that they play for a predetermined period of time or continually throughout the night. A number of these machines also include the sound of a heartbeat, which is often very effective in lulling newborns.

TODDLERS AND PRESCHOOLERS: TIME TO GET CREATIVE

As your baby matures into a toddler, the effectiveness of rocking begins to wane and parents need more creative techniques. For two- to three-year-olds, for instance, following a simple, consistent ritual is often necessary before sleep can be accepted and eventually achieved. Music, then, can serve as an instrumental, multipurpose part of the "sleepy-time" ceremony.

Sleepy-time Exercise #1
Making a personalized sleepy-time tape

> Step 1. Select about thirty minutes of your child's favorite soothing music that will, from this day forward, serve as his very own, personal and private "sleepy-time" music. Make these selections beforehand and present them to your child on the first night of this new routine so that he can "assist" you in formalizing these choices.

> Step 2. Play the same music, in the same order, at the same time, and at the same level, every night. Taping the selections to follow one another, back to back, is most effective and practical in the long run.

> Step 3. For three-year-olds, who often begin the ritual of getting up in the middle of the night and wandering around the house, keeping the

music playing throughout the night is sometimes helpful. You can do this by recording the same sequence of calming selections on both sides of the tape and playing it on an auto-reverse cassette player so that it will play continually. If you make this recording on a recordable compact disc, or mini-disc, simply activate the "continuous play" function on your player.

Sound Suggestion

For children who are unusually restless, or who complain of having "too many thoughts in my head," a metronome—a small timekeeping device used by musicians to help set and maintain a consistent tempo—can help. It can distract and relax the child by providing a slow, steady rhythm that captures his attention, and is often effective in quieting his thoughts.

Sleepy-time Exercise #2

Step 1. Reading to children during these early years is usually a very calming and natural part of the "sleepy-time" ritual. Select stories that have positive, comforting, and calming themes.

Step 2. Play soft music in the background as you read. Leaving the music on once the reading is concluded, and the kissing and tucking in are done, helps to maintain an ambience of safety and calm as the parent leaves the room. The music will also help to mask the noises the parent may make as he or she exits the bedroom and returns to other nighttime activities.

Step 3. An option to music is, again, the use of a sound machine. Involve your child in selecting which sound (e.g., waterfall, stream, rain, tropical rainforest, loons) she finds most soothing. Although she may prefer a different sound each night, the rule of "one sound for the night" should be firm and consistent.

Sleepy-time Exercise #3

Children between the ages of four and six frequently struggle with "bad dreams." Some will have problems in awakening from their dreams, or will wake screaming and find it very difficult to return to sleep. These children need a calm, reassuring parent to help comfort them back to sleep. Dreams of ghosts, wild animals, burglars, bad people, monsters under the bed, or numerous catastrophes may be reported. Music, again, can serve as a powerful ally in these situations.

Step 1. Select a number of soothing music pieces (see Music Menu 17, "Sleepy-Time Music") that you will use only for these "monster under the bed" occasions.

Step 2. During the first incident, tell your child that you have in your possession a tape of "special music" that will create good vibrations and help to chase, and keep, the bad dreams—along with the goblins and other troubling things—away.

Step 3. The use of music *in conjunction* with a parent's presence and reassurance will often be most effective in helping the child to return to sleep quickly.

Sound Suggestion

Use of a sound machine, as described earlier, will often help to quiet your child's mind or, again, block unwanted outside sounds. Set the machine to play continuously throughout the night to eliminate or minimize noise while also helping to "hush" your child's mind.

In general, always try to encourage your child to talk about her dreams. Listen attentively, being reassuring and supportive. Under no circumstances scold your child for these occurrences, accuse her of being a "baby," or threaten to punish her for her inability to fall asleep, for her night awakenings, or for her struggles with dreams or nightmares.

At around the age of six, children will increasingly benefit from a period of winding-down, alone time. This private time, during which they read or play with favorite toys, can be complemented with serene, soothing musical backgrounds. For a while, children in this age range will typically continue to enjoy a restful, pleasant chat with

Mom or Dad before going to sleep. Again, the use of music as a backdrop to a warm and receptive conversation assuring safety and positive outlooks can make a world of difference in your child's ability to fall, and stay, asleep.

The combination of using music as background to a spoken, progressive relaxation routine will help your child to relax his mind and body, and help him to drift off into sleep, often before the exercise is completed.* Although there are many good tapes that offer a number of deep muscle relaxation techniques with different types of music backgrounds, children sometimes prefer a parent's or older sibling's voice—and presence—guiding them through a relaxation routine. Scripted relaxation routines can be found in a number of stress reduction books (See General Resources, in Appendix B.) *The titles I have included in Music Menu 17—*It's Sleepy Time!*, and *Turning Day Dreams into Dreams: Bedtime Music*, are specifically designed for this purpose.

Children between the ages of seven and ten will benefit from an increasing amount of leeway and control in selecting their own music. At this age, some may have a favorite nighttime radio show that they like to listen to before going to sleep. Screen these shows for content to make sure they are acceptable for your children.

Sleepy-time Exercise #4

For this exercise, you will need a clock-radio or other similar time-setting sound device that can be used as a daily alarm. For example, cassette tape/CD combinations, or nature sound machines, that can be set in the same manner as regular alarm clocks, are available through catalogs and at department stores.

Step 1. Set your clock-radio (or alarm-clock device) to a station that specializes in playing soft music during these times.

Step 2. Regardless of the type of alarm-clock device you use, make sure your child awakens to soft, comforting sounds. Awakening to loud, raucous music in the morning is like being splashed with cold water.

Step 3. Once your child is awake, welcome him to the day with a positive greeting, such as asking if he had a good night's sleep and is ready for the day. How we wake up will help to set our vibrational state for the rest of the day.

Above all, be sound aware.

Music Menu #17
Sleepy-time music

It's Sleepy Time!	John M. Ortiz
Turning Day Dreams into Dreams: Bedtime Music	John M. Ortiz
Night Songs and Lullabies	Kim Scanlon
Rock-a-Bye Baby: Soft Hits for Little Dreamers	Disney
Smart Music! Sleepytime	Smart Music!
Butterfly Kisses and Bedtime Prayers, Vols. 1 and 2	Bob Carlisle
Dreamscapes: Lullabies from Around the World	Heidi Grant Murphy
Lullabies: 15 Soothing Songs for Babies	Susan McRae
Baby Sleep	Various Artists
Classical Baby: Mozart—Sleepy Time	Baby Tunes Mozart
Baby's Bedtime	Judy Collins
Barney's Sleepytime Songs	Barney
Bringing Up Baby (Vols. 1 and 3)	Joanie Bartels
Daddies Sing Good Night	Various Artists
Lullabies of Latin America (Spanish and English)	Maria Del Rey
Disney Lullaby Favorites	Various Artists
Dreamytime Songs	Sesame Street
Drift and Dream	Bear E. Sleepy
Bach at Bedtime: Lullabies for the Still of the Night (Set Your Life to Music Series)	Various Artists
Cajun Lullabies	Various Artists
Canyon Lullaby	Paul Winter
Dulcimer Lullabies	Joemy Wilson Young
Goodnight	Bronn Journey
Celtic Lullaby (Collection from Hearts of Space)	Various Artists
Sing Me to Sleep, Mommy	Various Artists
Lullaby Magic I & II	Joanie Bartels

Beethoven at Bedtime: A Gentle Prelude to Sleep	Set Your Life to Music Series
Jewish Lullabies	Various Artists
Lullaby	Arthur Fiedler
40 Winks	Jessica Harper
Dedicated to the One I Love	Linda Ronstadt
Sleep, Baby, Sleep	Nicolette Larson
African Lullaby	Various Artists
Getting Your Baby to Sleep, and Back to Sleep	Vicki Lansky

. . . and to help to gently awaken your child in the morning . . .

Baby's Morningtime	Judy Collins
Bringing Up Baby (Vol. 2)	Joanie Bartels
Smart Music! Playtime	Smart Music!
Classical Baby: Mozart—Awake Time	Baby Tunes Mozart
Songs to Brighten Your Day	Joe Scruggs & Dee Gibson

INTERMISSION

Top Ten Hits of Sound Awareness

As we engage in our daily "life dances," we tune in to various habits, some good, some bad, all of which slowly but surely shape our personalities, world views, and the ways in which we handle ourselves and interact with others. Once in a while, particularly when life events become hectic, and the pace begins to take a toll on our resources, we fall "out of tune," and our rhythms begin to lose their syncopation.

The following "Sound Awareness Sound Bytes" are offered to remind parents that even the finest instruments fall out of tune, and to provide ideas they may consider to assist them with composing harmonious patterns while nurturing their children.

SET THE TONE

From day one, set the tone for your family's interactions by never using profanity, using high volume sparingly, and speaking "with" or "to" rather than "at" your children. Avoid putting your children, or others, down, and eliminate all name-calling (e.g., "Why are you so *stupid*?!" "Are you listening, *numb*-brain?" "You're *worthless*!").

NAMES ARE VIBRATIONS WITH FACES

Each time you call out your child's name, say it consciously. Take a second and remind yourself that this is a precious life that you helped to create and bring into this world.

LISTEN TO YOUR CHILDREN

Active listening shows respect, and acknowledges others as valuable beings who are worthy of recognition.

BE POSITIVE

To the best of your ability, try to frame ideas, feelings, reminders, and other communications from a positive, proactive perspective. Even simple statements such as "I'm so tired" can be reframed into "This is a good time to take a break!" Always strive to find an encouraging, reassuring, optimistic angle.

READ TO YOUR CHILDREN
Your voice is your vibrational "soundprint"—it is unlike any other. Think of your voice as a nurturing tool.

STRIVE FOR HARMONY
When conflicts arise, aim to resolve, not to quibble or compete.

FINE-TUNE YOURSELF
Feel before you speak. When struggling with anger, anxiety or stress, think of yourself as an instrument that is temporarily out of tune. Would you continue to play an instrument that is out of tune? Before dispersing your negative emotions to your children, take a few seconds or a few minutes to fine-tune your instrument.

BE THE COMPOSER
In orchestrating family life, parents are the composers of a multi-dimensional symphony; each family member is a performer, and the entire world is your audience.

BE THERE THEN (OR HERE NOW!)
From the moment you become a parent, you are on stage, the lights are on, and the camera is rolling.

PLAY ON
Do not waste time and energy worrying about sour notes that have already been played. Parents and their children are works of art who are constantly in the process of becoming. We all make mistakes. Play on!

7
SELF-ESTEEM AND CONFIDENCE
Sounding Confident and Becoming Confidently Sound

Low self-esteem, in one or more of its many guises—poor self-confidence, self-identity, self-concept, self-worth, or self-respect—often leads to children's feelings of depression, stress, anger, or anxiety. It can lead anywhere from procrastination to total abandonment of projects, goals, and even lifelong dreams. Helping children develop positive self-esteem helps to instill a sense of responsibility and self-efficacy, and a healthy, positive internal sense of control (i.e., trust in their own abilities, self-reliance). By using music and sound in a number of creative ways, parents can help their children develop healthy self-identity, leading to positive self-esteem from day one. The purpose of this chapter is to provide parents with musical tools they can use to help their children gain self-assurance, enhancing the ability to believe in themselves.

> *As far back as I can remember, I've always struggled with low self-esteem. If I had to guess, I'd say that being a middle child in a family of talented overachievers had a lot to do with it. Being an average student, with minor—if any—athletic or artistic abilities, I always found myself hopelessly competing with my older sister, a superb athlete, and younger brother, who was the "brains" in the family.*
>
> *I remember one day I was feeling particularly down, so I grabbed my Walkman and went for a long walk. There I was, a romantic minstrel struggling to figure out who I was, and what I should do with my "average" life, and all of a sudden, this Hall and Oates song, "Do What You Want, Be What You Are" comes on the radio. The strangest thing, however, was that the DJ actually introduced the song by saying, "This next song will give you the key you've been looking for!"*
>
> *To this day I believe there was no way that was a coincidence. It really changed my perspective on the way I listen to music and*

*tune in to the powerful messages and vibrations songs can convey.
Soon afterward, I started to notice how many songs—"Rocky's
Theme," "Gonna Fly Now" by Maynard Ferguson, and "Go Your
Own Way" by Fleetwood Mac, for example—seemed to provide a
sort of emotional cushion and motivation for me to forge ahead
and accept myself for who I was. From that day forward, I started
the habit of choosing "personal message songs" that I would draw
from to help me get through just about any situation. I'm not saying that these songs "cured" me, but they have certainly been significant in helping me get through a lot of events more effectively.*

—Hunter, thirty-four, father of three, computer programmer

SELF-ESTEEM AND CONFIDENCE

- The youngest of three children, Mark often feels incapable of mea-
suring up to his older siblings, and tends to become discouraged by
the slightest setbacks, often giving up even as things start to go well.
- Joannie, a third grader with a beautiful singing voice, passes up
opportunities to take part in music-related school functions for fear
of rejection and the belief that she is "not good enough."
- Despite various achievements validating his many athletic abilities,
Dan's feelings of self-worth are so low that, despite being the top
hitter on his Little League team, he often refers to himself as either
"lucky" or "a loser."

The above situations illustrate issues that children with low self-
esteem deal with on a daily basis. In these and many similar situations, parents find themselves struggling for answers as to why their
children have developed such low self-esteem, and searching for
creative ways by which they can help to alleviate these problems.

INFANTS

The following musical suggestions are meant to provide a healthy
ambience of affirming, reassuring sound vibrations to help instill a
sense of positive self-worth.

(1) Invest in a reasonably good sound system that can be a permanent fixture in your child's room.

(2) Regularly play upbeat, happy tunes at moderate volumes.

(3) Diversify the musical backgrounds as much as possible, exposing your child to various World Music tunes, jazz, classics, etc. This will help to provide your child with a sound foundation based on different vibrational influences.

(4) Surround your child with songs that deliver active, positive messages.

TODDLERS AND PRESCHOOLERS

Following are a number of approaches and exercises that parents can consider for using music and sound to teach their young children some creative ways through which they may develop and enhance their positive self-esteem.

Sound self-esteem suggestions:

· Take time to sit down with your child and take turns selecting songs with uplifting, positive messages that you can *actively* listen to and discuss. Listen to his interpretation of the song with respect, offering supportive feedback on his observations. The interpretation of any art form, after all, is a very subjective and relative exercise. Encourage him to make personal choices, explore diversity, invent sounds, and create discoveries.

· If you are—or your child is—a budding musician, you may up the ante by playing selected tunes or encouraging her to take part in duets. Depending on her musical proficiency, "playing instruments" may consist of something as simple as tapping a beat on a tabletop and shaking a tambourine (or homemade equivalent) for rhythmic accompaniment. Other simple options are inexpensive electronic keyboards and synthesizers that can play virtual symphonies at the touch of a button!

· Make major events of taking your child on musical outings—jazz or Big Band shows, recitals or symphonies. Help to establish a sense of responsibility and self-worth by having him help choose which concerts he may prefer out of a series. Drive him to the ticket office to pick up the tickets, and while you're there, make a special effort to point out the colorful posters. Pick up brochures that describe the show. On concert night, you may choose to dress up, depending on the type of event and venue.

· Make a habit of renting classic as well as modern musicals selected together with your child. Complement and accentuate the weekly, bi-weekly, or monthly events by allowing him to also choose his favorite foods and sit on his favorite family chair.

· Enroll your child in music classes for a *favorite* instrument. Accomplishment of even minor feats, accompanied by regular acknowledgment of successes and efforts, will serve to further strengthen his self-esteem.

· Have your child join a musical group. Musical instruments can serve as excellent icebreakers, introducing shy children to social events. Being a contributing member of a group will further help to establish self-confidence and a positive self-identity.

Self-esteem-enhancing Exercise
Designer ditties

From a very early age, our names represent us. The vibrations that are emitted when we, or others, say our names can serve to reinforce the way that we perceive ourselves—they help to determine our self image, whether good or bad.

The following exercise is designed for toddlers and preschool age children, with the objective of instilling positive self-worth at an early age. Its purpose is to help your child develop original musical ditties that will serve to commend her name. Coming up with original compositions—regardless of how simple or silly these may sound—will help to personalize the tunes while giving her a sense of personal achievement, accomplishment, and self-worth.

Step 1. Help your daughter find some words that rhyme with her name. If her name is difficult to rhyme, then you may try placing it at the beginning or center of the tune. As you assist her with learning this process, take as little credit as possible for your contributions. Competition is not an issue in this exercise!

Step 2. If you have difficulty coming up with a melody for the song, try to choose one from among your daughter's, or your own, favorite *upbeat* (remember, the goal is to *raise* her self-esteem!) tunes that will lend itself to this purpose.

Step 3. As an example, you can choose a well-known tune, such as "Jingle Bells," to help guide your daughter through the process of coming up with a catchy tune that she may use as a musical affirmation. Try singing the following verse to the tune of "Jingle Bells":

> Jennifer, Jennifer,
> She's so very smart,
> She's so good at many things
> She tries with all her hea-rt!
> Jennifer, Jennifer,
> Talented and sweet,
> She's a truly special girl
> She's one that can't be beat!

Step 4. It is very important to allow your child to take part in as much of the process as possible, as this will serve to reinforce her own abilities. Also, be sure to applaud and compliment her for any efforts she makes that contribute *in any way* to this exercise!

Many of the exercises and ideas listed above for younger children will continue to effectively contribute to your maturing child's positive self-esteem. A parent's focus should continue to be on acknowledging positive attributes and encouraging a child's efforts and strengths.

Acknowledgment and praise for what may seem like a minor accomplishment (e.g., playing a neat piano scale, blowing a clean note out of a flute or saxophone, playing a drumbeat that sounds like something other than noise) will go a long way. Do not let your expectations get in the way of your child's natural path. Revel in his musical discoveries. Listen openly, providing silence to be filled by the sound.

Sound self-esteem suggestions:

· *Seize every opportunity to create harmony.* Frame your feedback comments in terms of positive affirmations (i.e., affirming self statements). Whatever your affirmations, however, be real. Children can
hear phony praise a mile away!

· *Encourage self-reliance.* As your child matures and grows nearer to
adolescence, he will continue to develop a sense of internal control. Consistent achievements in areas such as those described
above will help him to gradually develop a sense of self-worth and
independence.

· *Strive for balance.* Try to find a comfortable balance between allowing
your child to listen to the music she (and her peers) prefer during
these transitional periods, and monitoring these selections
to assure that they are acceptable to your family's belief systems
and standards. Keep in mind that your preadolescent daughter
is entering a *transition* period where much experimentation, and
social bonding, will be taking place. Don't lose sight of the changing times, peer influences, and media bombardment as to what is
"acceptable," and remember what your own parents thought about
your prepubescent musical tastes!

· *Let go of controlling attitudes.* Music is a very powerful force that is
often used to reflect one's own fantasy or perceived identity.
Compared to other forms of expression, music is a fairly safe
alternative. Allowing your son a certain level of control over
which music he can listen to during his "private time" may help to
avert other less desirable attempts at self-expression. Allowing
him to exercise his freedom of expression within reasonable limits will serve to model a sense of responsibility while encouraging
a locus of internal control. Listen, sort through available options,
and negotiate.

· *Hear music as an intergenerational bridge.* The music we choose to listen to almost always reflects our own "vibes." By realizing that your
daughter's chosen music may reflect how she feels at any given
moment, tuning in to this music will help you to further understand
the different "vibrational states" she is experiencing as she develops. In this manner, music may serve as a bridge for communicating

thoughts and feelings that she may be unable, or unwilling, to share through words.

Improving one's self-esteem is similar to improving one's musical abilities. Through hard work and practice, our ability to play our instrument, and to recognize our own worth, will become increasingly more natural and automatic.

POSITIVE SELF-ESTEEM GUIDELINES

The following guidelines are sound awareness raising suggestions that parents may share with their children to help enhance, and maintain, their levels of positive self-esteem as they deal with day-to-day life situations.

- Consider carefully the goals you set and try to make these realistic. Not every child will become a virtuoso.
- Encourage your school-age child to keep a journal, both audio and written, of *daily* successes. ("Today I played my first solo all the way through without making any mistakes!" "Today I learned the difference between flats, sharps and natural notes!")
- Place emphasis on *enjoying the process*. Listen to the sounds you create. Tune in to how the vibrations you bring to life in turn change your own vibrations and those of others around you.
- Listen to how your daily doses of *positive* self-talk become a way of "keeping yourself in tune."
- Encourage team participation and social *interaction*. Support play with a buddy or in a group.
- Actively listen to the expectations you have, or set, for your children. Tune in to *their* needs. *Respect* rather than *expect*.
- Maintain a *clean*, tidy practice environment that can serve as a quiet haven, or provide a space where your children can engage in sound exploration by singing, playing instruments, or simply "being children!"
- Encourage belief in natural abilities as well as individual *potential*.
- Listen regularly to music with *positive* messages and *uplifting* rhythms.

- Flaws, or "mistakes," present *opportunities for improvement*. They are reminders that we are human. When you hear flaws, help your children to place them in perspective.
- Learn to use humor as a counter to self-deprecation: "Wow, I think I just invented a new note!" "I bet that sound will be really popular in the future!"
- Listen to life, be sound-aware of the process. Play each note *one at a time* (unless you're playing chords!).
- If a particular instrument, or type or music, does not feel right, *try another*.
- If a particular music teacher does not complement *your own* vibrations, try to find someone else who does. *Compatibility* makes a world of difference in defining one's self-image.
- Take an active interest in your child's favorite music and musicians. Sitting with your child through a few minutes of "the video I've been talking about!" or "the song I really want you to hear!" will provide priceless, quality opportunities to bond with your children. If the song or video is of an acceptable nature, be sure to mention something *supportive* and *genuinely* positive: "Those are some great harmonies!" or, "I can see why you're so excited about this group, is this their first video?" or, "What a great rhythm section!" (A "rhythm section" is usually a bass guitar and drums.)
- Finish every practice session by playing a *favorite* tune.
- Finally, act like a detective. There's a positive note to *everything* ... find it! Support, encouragement and praise are wonderful self-esteem fertilizers. As the old song goes: "Accentuate the positive."

Music Menu #18
Sound self-esteem

You Are Special	Mr. Rogers
You Can Do It If You Try	Bingo and Molly
Did I Ever Tell You How Lucky You Are?	Dr. Seuss
Valdy's Kids Record	Valdy
Help Yourself!	Kathy Fink and Marcy Marxer
I Am Proud To Be Me	Teddy Ruxpin

Positively Positive Day	Todd Oliver
It's Another Positively Positive Day	Todd Oliver
Peace Is the World Smiling: A Peace Anthology	Various Artists
Minnie and Me: Songs Just for Girls	Various Artists
Smile	Tia
Tickles You	Rosenshontz
Dinner Alone Is a Bore!	Danny Einbender and Friends
Songs for the Inner Child	Shaina Noll
Building Self-Esteem	Rock 'N Learn
Free To Be You and Me	Marlo Thomas and Friends
Building Character	Twin Sisters

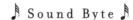

♪ Sound Byte ♪

Every morning, when you wake up,
Set your dial to "worthwhile."

8

EXPLORING OUR ROOTS AND RHYTHMS

Grandpa's Tales and Grandma's Feather Bed

Grandparents have license to spoil us. Having paid their dues by raising Mom and Dad, they are now free to be kids once again, but with all the grownup experience! They're the only ones who can get away with giving us a cookie *before* supper, and admiring how much we've grown, even if they see us every day. Having planted the seeds that became our parents, our grandparents are the very roots of our family rhythms.

Some of my fondest memories, those that rank somewhere between a smile on my face and a tear in my eye, involve time traveled and moments shared with my grandparents. Not to brag, but my grandfather's tall tales were as alpine as my grandmother's home-cooked meals were culinary works of art. It is unfortunate that many children experience life with very little to no contact with their grandparents. Who else, for instance, can we trust to give us the inside story on Mom's first "love crush," or imitate the way that Dad—who had to sleep with a night light until the age of fourteen—used to lower his voice whenever he talked to girls on the phone?

(Note: The following exercise need not be limited to those children fortunate enough to have a close relationship with a grandparent. A significant, surrogate elderly person who may be part of a child's life, such as an older aunt or uncle, or a close family friend, could perhaps fit the mold close enough to participate in certain parts of this exercise.)

There comes a time in every child's life when he or she begins to wonder about his or her family history. What are my origins? Who were my ancestors, where did they come from, what were they like? What were their interests, their dreams, their accomplishments?

Take advantage of the fact that grandparents can often help to revive old memories, often embellishing them with entertaining anecdotes. The following exercise is designed to help children bond with their grandparents while developing and expanding their sound awareness of their ancestral stories.

Exercise #1
Interviewing our past

Materials needed: tape, mini-disc or other type of audio recorder

Ages: preschool and school-age children

Step 1. First and foremost, discuss the planned event with Grandma and Grandpa and make sure you have their support, understanding, and interest in taking part in this exercise.

Step 2. Present the idea of making this family "interview tape" to your children as a potentially exciting, special activity. Make a point of how fortunate they are to be able to engage in an adventure involving one or more of their grandparents.

Step 3. Over a period of about a week, suggest to your children that they think of some questions they may have about *their* own personal pasts that their grandparents may be able to answer. These may include events that took place at some point early on in their lives and which Grandma and Grandpa may be able to clarify or expand upon.

Step 4. Although parents may know the answers, and may have already shared some of these bits of information with their children, it is often fun for them to hear a different perspective. Encourage your children to come up with their own questions and to write them down in a notebook as they occur.

If the children are having problems coming up with specific questions, parents can help them. Rather than outlining particular questions, the parents may initiate interest by suggesting broad categories that may encourage the children to design their own sets of questions. Suggestions may include: place where you grew up, favorite foods or toys, special events, holidays, funny moments, etc.

If they are still having problems, you may suggest more specific questions, such as:

· Do you remember when I was born?
· What was I like when I was a baby?
· What were some of the funny things that I used to do?
· Did we play any special games?
· What are some good holiday or birthday stories from the "old" days?

The goal of the questions is not so much to obtain information or facts as it is to give the grandparents an opportunity to reminisce about events that may be of interest to themselves as well as to the children. It is also aimed at giving the children a starting point from which they can initiate a dialogue with their grandparents.

Other questions could involve stories about the parents.

· What was Mom like when she was a little girl?
· What things did she like to do?
· What were some funny things Mom did when she was my age?
· What types of clothes did she wear to school? How about her hair-style? (This is an excellent time to bring out those old high school yearbooks!)
· Who were some of Mom's friends?
· What did you think of Daddy when you first met him?
· Did Mom have other boyfriends?
· What was Mom and Dad's wedding like? (Again, great time for pictures, slides, or old family films.)

Once the list is complete, have your children phone, or perhaps send an e-mail or other correspondence, to their grandparents to schedule a date for the interview. This will help to formalize the event and provide it with an air of importance and authenticity.

Help your children set up a date when they can sit down with their grandparents for a certain length of time and tape the interview. The length of the interview depends on many factors, including your child's age and attention span, and the grandparents' health. While ten to fifteen minutes may be all that a first or second grader needs, older children will typically need longer periods of time. Just in case, set aside one hour, which should suffice, particularly if you have a set of questions already prepared.

Once they have come up with questions about themselves and their own upbringing, suggest to your children that they also develop questions about their grandparents and *their* lives. Some examples may include:

- Where were you born?
- Where did you go to school? Which subjects did you study there?
- Who were some of your best friends? What games did you play?
- What types of clothes did you wear? (Grandparents could embellish their stories by showing old photographs.)
- What were your first jobs?
- How, where, and when did you and Grandma (Grandpa) meet and fall in love?
- What were some of your hobbies?
- Did you play any sports or participate in any other organized activities?
- What was your favorite music? Who were your favorite artists? (Grandparent could offer to play some of the old songs and discuss the journey from vinyl to cassettes, CDs, etc.)
- What did you originally want to be when you grew up?

By planning, discussing, and carrying out the above exercise, your children will be engaging in a number of processes that will help to raise their sound awareness. The mere acts of choosing the "right" questions, presenting (asking) them, and listening to a response that is personally pertinent to ourselves often helps us to tune in a bit more actively and attentively. Also, by raising awareness of their family's history, the children will gain a deeper understanding of their ancestry, forever altering the ways in which they look at, and listen to, themselves and their extended family. Further, from a sound awareness perspective, the children will come away with fresh knowledge regarding a number of old artists and musical periods, that will hopefully help to tweak their interest, and broaden their understanding of different types of music.

Aside from raising sound awareness and exposing your children to learning about different types of music and artists, this exercise also provides an excellent opportunity for all parties to reconnect and strengthen their bonds. In addition, your children will be collecting a priceless "audio memento" of various significant people in their lives that may, one day, greatly complement old photographs and help to trigger irreplaceable memories.

I recently spoke with a gentleman, presently in his mid-forties, who related that, on his twenty-first birthday, his parents gave him a special gift. As he was growing up, he indicated, they had cautiously kept a record of sounds that carried special significance throughout his development. This gift, a personal "audio-graph," triggered memories of long-forgotten sounds that recalled many special, long-forgotten events. Among these were his father teaching him a favorite tune at age four, a recital at age seven, a hit tune from the soundtrack to his first favorite movie, and his name being announced at the high school auditorium during his graduation. Twenty-odd years later, now a highly educated, highly successful, content, and fulfilled family man, he still considers this loving memento the greatest birthday gift of his life.

Recently, during a family reunion, he presented his own children with their own audio-graphs detailing their respective developmental sound milestones. By helping to raise their sound awareness, he has increased the chances that a family tradition will continue to evolve.

Exercise #2
Family audio-graphs: making musical time capsules

The objective of this exercise is to collect a number of sounds that will help capture the present in sound form, much as a photograph or video helps to preserve it visually.

This is a very flexible exercise, in that once the basic concept is understood, parents may use it in a number of different ways. Two different types of audio-graphs are presented here.

Materials needed: a tape recorder, disc recorder, or other audio-recording device; audiotape, recordable disc, or other audio-recording software.

Although an audio-graph can be started *at any time* during a person's history, the example illustrated here gives suggestions for sounds that parents can begin to record at the very beginning of a child's life.

- Begin by recording the heartbeat of your baby in the womb. These can be obtained fairly easily with the assistance of your physician.
- Record the first cries emitted by your baby at the moment of birth.
- Keeping the tape recorder near the crib, record vocal advances made by your infant during the process of preverbal development (e.g., cooing, gurgling, babbling, lalling, echoing sounds, crying, squealing, etc.)
- The magical "first word" (although it will be nearly impossible to catch the actual first word, phrase, etc., the objective is to try to catch these early verbalizations on tape as they begin to surface).
- Laughter.
- Special words ("Mommy," "Daddy," "water," etc.).
- First (or early) phrase.
- First musical attempts.
- "No!"
- "Yes!"
- First phone call (recorded from home).
- Other first phone call (recorded from the *other* end. This can be done as the child calls from Grandma's, or by a parent who calls while away on a business trip).
- First birthday party sounds.
- Alphabet song recital.
- Singing first favorite jingle.
- First favorite nursery tune.
- Early attempt at "conversation."
- First favorite pop song (record one version right off the actual recording and a second with your child singing along with it).
- Favorite song from first movie soundtrack watched.
- Theme song from favorite early television show.
- Heart-to-heart session.
- Grandma's and Grandpa's voices.
- Siblings' and other relatives' voices. Have them perhaps share a personal greeting or special message.
- Singing recital(s) at school, church or other organized event.
- Etceteras!

As you can see, a developmental audio-graph can begin from—literally—day one and proceed through the mazes, mountains, rivers, and valleys of your child's monumental (or not so very monumental) sound experiences. A number of suggestions:

- It is strongly suggested that you be economical and tape these events sparingly as you save them for posterity. Those among us with boxes and boxes of unsorted old photographs know exactly what I mean!
- Always label.
- Keep a running record of events as you record them…now, not later!
- Always remove the safety tab on your audiotape once the tape is filled. The last thing you want to do is erase over the past!
- Make a copy. With all of the affordable technologies today for quality audio reproduction, I suggest that sounds be transferred, on a regular basis, to a safe backup system, whether it be another analog tape source, disc format, or computer-related digital format (e.g., DAT).

Saved for posterity, audio-graphs can be preserved and handed down from generation to generation. As in the story of the gentleman related above, these personal soundtracks can raise our sound awareness across generations.

Above all, have fun!

Exercise #3
A Day in a Life audio-graph: having a sound day

The goal of this exercise is to collect a number of sounds during the course of one full day that will serve as a sound representation to be played back at a later period in your child's—or your—life. Although most of the suggestions presented can be used with children of different ages, parents may want to modify some of them according to their child's present, age-relevant capabilities.

- Try to select a time when you will be available for at least most of the day so that you can assist your child in the collection of sounds. Remember, this is not merely a day during which you will take a few minutes to record some sounds "here and there," but rather a planned, anticipated *quality* day in your parent-child life—a "keepsake day."
- Make the day an event! A week or so before the actual event, introduce it to your child, discussing the main idea (to collect and record

sounds), materials you will use, and some of the suggestions you may have. Ask your child to spend time during the next few days thinking of sounds to record, and to jot them down.

- If you use any particular sounds (phrases such as "Time to get up, Honey," or clock radio) to wake your child, you may want to begin with taping those sounds. If your child gets up before you do (which is the case in many households) you can start the tape by recording a mutual morning greeting: "Good morning, how are you? Do you remember what day this is?"

- If your child typically watches a special morning television show or cartoon you may then record a few seconds of the characters' voices, the theme song, and perhaps even one or two of the commercials in between.

- Sit together for breakfast and discuss your plans for the day. Once you've got the day outlined, turn on the recorder and take turns summarizing your game plan.

- Play a game. Record some of the interaction. If your child is a toddler, this step may require that you take a greater role in initiating the questions and prompting responses. If your child has musical toys available, it may be a good idea to focus on playing with these for a while, recording the sounds the toys make along with your child's interactive dialogues.

- Go on a "sound hunt." If you live in the country this should be a cinch. Simply step out and collect as many nature sounds as you can find. If you live in the suburbs or the city, this may be a good day to drive out to the country, the beach, or a park. For more specific ideas on sound hunts, see Sound Hunting: Sound Safari in chapter 9.

- Make phone calls. Record phone calls to special people in your child's life: Grandma, Grandpa, aunts, cousins, siblings living away from home. (Please remember to always obtain the other person's permission prior to recording the conversation.)

- Include older siblings. If there are older siblings in the home, make sure that they are included on the tape, even if all they have to say is "This is really stupid!"

- Make short visits. Take a walk or a ride to visit some of your child's friends and record greetings or comments from each of them.

- Have regular "check-ins" throughout the day, when you flip on the recorder and have short chats with your child, or children, asking if they have any particular thoughts or feelings they would like to share.
- While in the car making visits, or traveling to and from some designated place to record, turn on the radio. If a favorite song comes on, record it, and encourage an impromptu sing-along. An alternative is to bring along a current or favorite tape or CD and record at least one sing-along on the way.
- Back home, you may consider recording one or two "bubble-bath tunes." This may be done together, or, if your child is now old enough to bathe alone, you can allow him to do this on his own. However, you may want to help monitor the taping. Be sure your child is absolutely safe—use a battery-powered device and keep it far away from the water (see end of chapter for recommended "bubble-bath tunes").
- If your family typically watches television in the evening, record a theme song, some commercials, and a few seconds of some favorite characters' dialogue.
- As the time to retire for the day approaches, sit down with your child and—with recorder rolling—discuss your thoughts and feelings regarding the day's events. Record a typical "tucking in" routine with you—or your child—reading a bedtime story, singing lullabies, or playing music to lull your child to sleep.
- Don't forget to leave enough room for your "Goodnight, sleep tight, don't let the bed bugs bite!" or "Have sweet dreams!" variation.

♪ Sound Byte ♪

In the end,
remember to have a sound day!

Sound resources recommended for nurturing your child's cultural roots:

Music Menu #19
Family tunes

Family Tree	Tom Chapin
Grandfather's Greatest Hits	David Holt

Pete Seeger's Family Concert	Pete Seeger
Home: Volume 1	Various Artists
Songs From a Parent to a Child	Art Garfunkel
This Land Is Your Land	Woody Guthrie

Music Menu #20
American classics

The following classic American standard tunes are recommended as some that might be appealing to children while serving to inspire family values and cultural awareness.

Ac-cent-tchu-ate the Positive	Harold Arlen
America the Beautiful	Katharine Lee Bates and Samuel A. Ward
A-Tisket, A-Tasket	Ella Fitzgerald
Camptown Races	Stephen Foster
Cheek to Cheek	Fred Astaire
Clementine	Pete Seeger
Dancing on the Ceiling	Rodgers and Hart
Don't Sit Under the Apple Tree	Andrews Sisters
Fascinating Rhythm	George Gershwin
Get Happy	Harold Arlen
God Bless America	Kate Smith
God Bless the Child	Billie Holiday
Goodnight, Sweetheart	Rudy Vallee
I Got Rhythm	Ethel Merman
It's a Grand Night for Singing	Rodgers and Hammerstein
Mammy	Al Jolson
Oh, What a Beautiful Morning	Rodgers and Hammerstein
Ol' Man River	Jerome Kern
Sonny Boy	Al Jolson
Take Me Out to the Ballgame	Jack Norworth and Albert von Tilzer
Take the "A" Train	Duke Ellington
The Battle of New Orleans	Jimmy Driftwood
This Land Is Your Land	Woody Guthrie
Toot Toot Tootsie	Eddie Cantor
Up a Lazy River	Hoagy Carmichael

When the Moon Comes Over the Mountain	Kate Smith
You'll Never Walk Alone	Rodgers and Hammerstein
You're the Top	Cole Porter
Patriotic Songs & Marches	Kimbo Educational
American Folk Songs	Pete Seeger
American Heroes	Jonathan Sprout
American Children (various artists)	Alacazam
Kids Sing America (various artists)	Brentwood Kids
Wee Sing America	Wee Sing

Music Menu #21
Multicultural diversity

The following titles are recommended for introducing children to the sounds and rhythms of diverse cultures. Although some are in English, many are sung in their original tongues, helping to also introduce foreign languages as part of original, musical packages.

African Songs & Rhythms for Childhood	Various Artists
African Songs & Rhythms for Children	Various Artists
American Folk Songs for Children	Mike and Peggy Seeger
Anna Moo Crackers (Latin, African and Cajun influences)	Anna Moo
Cajun for Kids	
Choo Choo Boogaloo (Creole music)	Buckwheat Zydeco
Dance to Your Daddy (Celtic)	Teresa Doyle
El Lobo: Songs and Games of Latin America (as sung by children)	Various Artists
Fiesta Musical: A Musical Adventure Through Latin America for Children in English and Spanish	Emilio Delgado
Gi'me Elbow Room: Folk Songs from a Scottish Childhood	Bonnie Rideout
Irish Ballads and Songs of the Sea	Various Artists
Irish Folk Tales for Children	Sharon Kennedy
Joining Hands with Other Lands	Kimbo Educational
Kwanzaa Music: A Celebration of Black Cultures in Song	Various Artists
Multicultural Children's Songs	Ella Jenkins

Multicultural Rhythm Stick Fun	Georgiana Stewart
My Jewish Discovery	Craig Taubman
My Newish Jewish Discovery	Craig Taubman
Papa's Dream (Mexican-American influences)	Los Lobos and Lola Guerrero
Prophecy: A Hearts of Space Native American Compilation	Various Artists
Songs About Native Americans	Lois Skiera Zuceck
Tales From the First World: Stories and Songs from Africa, Haiti & America	Synia and Jeff McQuillan
Teach the Children: A Tribute to African-American History	T Medicine May YaYa
The Celtic Cradle	Jill Rogoff
The World Sings Goodnight 1 & 2	Various Artists
Under the Green Corn Moon—Native American Lullabies	Various Artists

SOUND RESOURCES RECOMMENDED FOR NURTURING YOUR CHILD IN THE TUB

Music Menu #22
Bubble-bath tunes

Bathtime Magic	Joanie Bartels
Bathtub Blues	Greg Brown
Splish, Splash: Bath Time Fun	Sesame Street
Singin' in the Bathtub	John Lithgow
Bathtime	Bear E. Sleepy

9

FRIENDS MAKE WONDERFUL DANCE PARTNERS

Regardless of the amount of time, love, and support that parents give their children, ongoing, positive relations with friends offer a dimension that extends beyond their immediate family's umbrella. The challenges and rewards that come with building, developing, and maintaining complementary relations with same-age peers provide a foundation for the invaluable tools your children will continue to hone and expand upon throughout their lives.

In our society, as in many others, music functions as a sort of "magnet" and "anchor" for communal activities. Most children find it difficult to walk past a community center, park, neighbor's yard, or even an ordinary room where music is setting an upbeat, festive tone. When they hear others singing, children either naturally join in, even if simply by echoing or humming the lyrics, or otherwise stop in their tracks and focus attentively, captivated by the harmonies and sounds. At parties, music helps children (and adults, for that matter) to come together by removing a number of invisible barriers. Background music, for example, immediately eliminates periods of uncomfortable silence. If it is relaxing, it gives us an "excuse" to be peaceful together, and if it is stimulating it then frees us to dance, jump around, and even act silly in ways we would not otherwise do. If nothing else, it gives us something tangible that is being shared at that moment which can be discussed—the music itself. A single song, regardless of its genre or style, can act as a wonderful springboard for children to begin discussing their own musical leanings and preferences. Having "broken the ice," they are now ready to embark into other areas of personal sharing, with the music opening up opportunities for bonding and social interaction. Further, while helping to raise awareness of the world in which they live, music helps to give children a glimpse into the past, inspiring them to develop ideas that will evolve throughout their lifetimes.

Our home is pretty much acknowledged as the neighborhood's equivalent of a "community center" and we wouldn't have it any other way. It's always given our three kids, Michael (twelve), Allyson (ten), and Jacob (seven) plenty of opportunities to socialize, share, and learn from other children. We both grew up in small apartments in the city, and one of our main priorities we had after getting married was to settle down in a place that would give our kids plenty of room to run free and have their own space, both indoors and out. The other thing we wanted to provide for them was the opportunity to explore music and pursue their creative talents. In both instances, it's turned out better than we could have ever imagined. Our back yard alone is larger than the "park" my parents used to take us to when we were kids. As far as the music goes, little by little we've turned our entire basement into an amazing playroom/recording studio/disco. The whole downstairs is equipped with musical instruments, video camera, four-track recording studio, "dance floor," and even a stage where all of the neighborhood children come to sing Karaoke, party, and play musical games. Sometimes I go down there while the kids are asleep, look around, and think of the wonderful memories my children will be taking into their adult lives.

—Lauren, thirty-four, real-estate agent

MUSICAL GAMES AND GROUP ACTIVITIES

As social beings, one of the greatest gifts that parents can give their children is the opportunity to develop relationships with peers. In music, parents have a fun, practical, and versatile ally that they can use to engage their children in social activities, and expose them to situations where they may explore their interpersonal needs and practice their social skills. Music gives us a safe, comfortable and universal reason to come together if simply just to share the musical experience.

The general purpose of all of the following exercises, which are designed to help develop and strengthen peer and social relations, is discussed below:

(1)   To provide creative ways of spending quality time with our children while also teaching them proper ways of social interaction.

(2)   To teach both parents and children ways of enjoying the process of raising their sound awareness by participating in fun activities with family and friends.

(3)   To participate and collaborate together in a number of activities that will have both primary (immediate) and secondary (long-term) gains.

(4)   To nurture our children's friendships with other children, helping them to develop skills that will enhance their lives and social skills.

Exercise #1
The sound collage

The idea of a sound collage can be introduced by Mom or Dad as a one-day project or as a long-term undertaking.

Purpose: To collect thoughts, impressions, ideas and feelings from friends or relatives that your children will be able to listen to many years from now. Sound collage copies also make wonderful gifts that can be given to the participants.

Materials needed: Portable tape recorder (or other recording device), blank tape, batteries.

Ages: Six to twelve.

Timeline suggestions
Short-term options:
· During a party or sleep-over when lots of friends are together.
· As a school project over a class period.
· On the way back from a class trip.
· Family get-togethers, or during a holiday when many family members are available.
· New Year's Eve party.
· School graduation/end of school year.

Long-term options:
- Over summer vacation as your family visits a number of relatives.
- Over a long holiday break during which relatives and friends are visited.
- During summer camp when many new friendships are developed.
- As a school project over the course of a semester, or even during the school year.

General ideas for topics

Suggest to your child that he or she first explain the purpose of this project and then get permission from people before getting their interviews on tape.

Assuming that you've chosen an occasion when a number of people have come together for a common purpose, your child can follow a number of angles. One such angle may be to ask those willing to participate if they would like to offer any comments or share feelings about simply "being there" (in other words, what it is like for them to be at this gathering). A second angle is one based on themes. Themes can be developed and questions can revolve around some of the following suggested general concepts.

Theme ideas

- Summer camp: How does it feel to be away from home for six weeks? What would you say are your three favorite things about being here?
- Holiday: What does this particular holiday mean to you?
- Family get-together: Can you share any particularly funny, family-related stories from the past?
- School play: What has been the best part about being part of this play?
- School project: What are some of the things you are most enjoying as we work on this project? What parts of this project are your least favorite?
- School graduation/end of school year: What will you miss most about this class? What were three things you learned this year that you think will help you in the future?
- New Year's Eve party: What were some of this year's highlights for you? Have you made any resolutions for the New Year?

Some general reminders

(1)   Always introduce the main topic area and month/year (i.e., summer camp, 2001; New Year's Day, millennium) at the beginning of each tape.

(2)   Always label the tape or CD!

(3)   Always introduce the person being interviewed by name and state where the person lives ("I'm now talking with my buddy Frank, from Ashland, Virginia"), or have the person introduce herself or himself as you begin the recording ("Could you introduce yourself and tell us where you're from?").

(4)   Once the recording is completed, always remove the safety tab from the tape to ensure that it is not accidentally erased later on!

(5)   It is your option as to whether you want to promise each participant a copy of the tape or simply surprise them at a later time (personally, I vote for the surprise!).

Exercise #2
Stormy Night In

Purpose: An opportunity for bonding with friends, siblings, and family members while raising sound awareness.

Materials needed: Flashlight, a few dripless candles, snacks.

Ages: Eight to twelve.

It's Friday night and nine-year-old Amy's highly anticipated soccer game has been cancelled due to especially bad weather. It is storming, raining, with thunder and lightning and even a little hail thrown in for effect. Suddenly, Amy and her two best friends and teammates are sequestered at her home, where they had planned a sleepover. Fortunately, Amy's dad, who is sound-aware enough to welcome the wonderful opportunity being presented by Mother Nature, suggests the idea of a "Stormy Night In!"

> Step 1. Raid the refrigerator and kitchen shelves and make yourself a virtual buffet of everything that seems tantalizing. Everything's game! In particular, this is a great time to create a homemade pizza, bake some

bread, or put together a batch of "magical cookies." (My own personal "magical cookie" recipe includes chocolate chips, walnuts, and raisins. The only "magical" thing about these recipes is that each person gets to choose his or her own ingredients and go hog wild!) If the electricity is temporarily out due to the storm, make do with store-bought cookies, chips, and peanut butter sandwiches.

Once the eating is done it's time to begin!

Step 2. Using the flashlights, find your way to a room in your home where the outside sounds are loudest; this may be a patio, attic, den, or any other room where the gang can make itself comfortable. Turn off the flashlights and simply begin to tune in to the sound concert.

Step 3. Focus first on the cacophony of the event: the totality of sounds and lights being brought to you by Nature herself. The pouring rain, the combination of rhythms as water cascades off the roof and gushes through the gutters. The random blasts and rumbles of thunder. The wind battering and rocking the trees. The trees creaking and swaying. Tune in to how the whole is so much greater than the sum of its parts.

Step 4. Listen carefully. Focus on how the sound of the pouring rain tends to quiet your mind. Listen to how, by yielding to the relentless sounds, your thoughts tend to stray and you are left with a sense of being part of a vast, sound universe.

Step 5. Next, try to pick out one single, solitary sound. This could be the constant dripping of single water drops that have somehow managed to elude the barrage of the moment. A single, persistently individual sound that, in spite of the competition, manages to stand out if only in a subtle way. It might be the creaking of an isolated tree branch, or a faint whistle that seems to come and go from every which way, or maybe from nowhere at all!

Listen carefully to how the sounds make you feel. Listen to the thoughts that go through your mind, the stories that your mind begins to create.

[Children ages ten to twelve, can continue here, or try the option for older children described below]

After listening for about ten to fifteen minutes, light the candles. Take turns going around the room and have each person share his and her feelings about their experiences of listening to the rain, other sounds, and to themselves.

Once the group is done exchanging stories, it might already be time to go to bed. If not, blow out the candles and repeat the exercise. But if it's time to go to bed, crack a window open just enough so that you can continue to hear the sounds, and flow with the storm as it lulls you to sleep.

[Option for children ages ten to twelve]

Try listening to the thoughts and feelings that you are having about listening to the rain. About sitting in the dark, safely within a small circle of friends (and family) and the special moment that you are sharing with them.

As you focus on the one, specific sound source, think of someone close to you who may—for some reason—remind you of this one sound that has such a unique personality all its own. A person who follows his or her own path, who, while seeming to blend in with the crowd, also manages to keep his or her own individuality. The person might just be sitting right next to you in the room at this moment, or could be many miles away, perhaps even thinking about you.

Think of some of the positive qualities that this person has, and the influences that he or she may have had in your life. Think of at least one positive effect that this person has had in your life.

After listening for about twenty to thirty minutes, light the candles. Take turns going around the room and have everybody share their feelings about listening to the rain, and to themselves. Talk about the person whom the sounds brought to mind, and the positive feelings you have about that person.

Exercise #3
A musical gift

Greeting cards offer many different "personal" messages for various reasons. Most people, for example, either do not have the time to come up with their own, original messages in poetic form, or are not able to come up with a message that they consider satisfactory in terms of expressing their feelings or thoughts toward another person.

For those of us who prefer to compose our own messages, however, blank greeting cards are available. Likewise, for those of us who are music lovers, blank tapes (or recordable DATs, CDs or mini discs) are conveniently accessible.

Purpose: To make a personal gift that either conveys the way you feel about another person, or offers messages—and vibrations—that you want to communicate to someone special.

Materials needed: Tape recorder, DAT or CD recorder, blank tape, music collection.

Ages: Eight to twelve. (Younger children can do this with their parents' assistance.)

Step 1. Over a period of a few days, take some time to put together a list of songs from your collection which you feel either express how you feel about the person to whom you want to give this gift ("This is what you mean to me"), or which convey any number of other personal messages ("Hang in there, you'll get through this").

Another possibility is a song compilation that has symbolic meaning for the two of you, such as songs you've shared over the past year or two, or those that remind you of special events you may have shared at some point in your life.

Step 2. Once the songs are decided upon, arrange them in the order you feel will best reflect your intention. For instance, a song that reminds you of when you first met should go first, followed by other songs as they reflect different feelings or bonding events in your lives.

Step 3. Having selected all of the songs you would like to record on this tape, list them in order. Using the liner notes or song listings, look up the total time for each song and write it next to each number you plan to record. Add up all of the song times, then add about six to eight seconds for every "in between" segment, and make sure that the total time will fit comfortably onto your tape or CD.

FRIENDS MAKE WONDERFUL DANCE PARTNERS

The above approach is very helpful because, although it will take a little extra time up front, it will save you an enormous amount of work in the long run. If you do not have enough songs to make a full tape, you may want to either add more songs or purchase a shorter-length tape. If your song list exceeds the time length of the tape, you can either purchase a longer tape or remove some songs. You can also use both sides of the tape.

Although there is nothing wrong with filling up half a tape with, say, four or five songs that properly convey the message, most people prefer to have a full tape. If you want the tape to be filled with music, one option is to record the songs you choose and then fill up the rest of the tape with appropriate instrumental music.

Step 4. Having completed your personalized "musical gift," wrap it with love and share it with a loved one.

PARTY TIME/SLEEP-OVER/HOLIDAY MUSICAL GAMES

Exercise #1
What's That Song?!

Purpose: To generate group interaction and promote team play; to learn about new songs and artists through friends' music collections.

Materials needed: Moderate-sized box or bag. Audiotapes and CDs brought in by each child. Sound system that can play both tapes and CDs. (Suggestion: Since CDs can be easily "cued" from song to song, it is strongly recommended that you use CDs for this game whenever possible).

Ages: Four to twelve.

Step 1. While passing out invitations to your child's party or sleep-over, request that each guest bring three or four favorite tapes or CDs of popular or children's music. Be sure to tell the children that they are not to tell anyone which tapes or CDs they are choosing to bring in!

Step 2. As the children arrive at the party, the supervising adult collects the tapes and CDs and places them in a box or bag.

Step 3. The party host also contributes three or four of his or her favorite song collections.

Game rules

The rules are explained by a parent, host or older sibling once all guests are present. It is advised that a supervising adult handle the duties of selecting and playing the songs that will be played at this party. That person is called the "DJ."

Step 1. The DJ indicates that he or she is going to play the first song. No other hints are given. The DJ then chooses a song at random from the many tapes and CDs brought in by the guests and contributed by the host.

Step 2. The first number is played. As soon as someone thinks she or he knows the song, they raise their hand and call out. The CD or tape is put on "pause." That person then ventures their guess.

Step 3. If the guess is wrong, the song continues to be played until either someone identifies it or until the song is finished. A song is "correctly identified" if someone can name the title. If the guess is correct, the person earns points based on the chart below.

Step 4. If a song cannot be identified, then no one gets credit for that song, and they move on to a different song from a separate CD or tape. Once everyone gives up on a particular song, however, it is identified by the DJ, and that song is no longer played. Other songs from that same CD, however, can be tried later.

Points are obtained in the following manner:
- Correctly naming the song in five seconds or less = five points.
- Correctly naming the song in ten seconds or less = four points.
- Correctly naming the song in twenty seconds or less = three points.
- Correctly naming the song in thirty seconds or less = two points.
- Correctly naming the song before it is over = one point.

Bonus points are gathered as follows:
- Correctly naming the song's artist, after correctly identifying a song = three points.

- One bonus point can be earned by naming other songs that are part of each particular CD or tape.

    If the person tries to guess other songs on a particular CD or tape but ends up naming a tune that is not part of that collection, that person loses a point and the DJ moves on to the following song.

Sound Suggestion

The person who brings in the CD from which the song is being played cannot venture a guess about that CD!

Exercise #2
Television show-theme Charades

Purpose: To exercise the memory via recollection of melodies. To provide interaction between family members and friends.

Materials needed: Television program guide. Tape recorder.

Ages: Four to twelve.

Step 1. Take a recent television guide and go through the weekly programs, writing down any recent family favorites that feature catchy theme songs or tunes. You may need to wait until the shows are on during the week to refresh your memory on particular tunes.

Step 2. As you scan the guide, also pay special attention to older shows, no longer on prime time, with theme songs that your family would recognize. Be sure to include cartoons and other programs your children watch. Add these to the list.

Step 3. When the theme songs come on, record and list them in order, naming the shows they are from. If your recorder has a counter, make sure you start the tape on "zero" and take note of where each theme song is recorded on the tape. This will be a tremendous advantage if you wish to search for a particular song later on!

Step 4. Write out the names of the shows on individual strips of paper and place them in a box or bag (OK, or a hat!)

During your next family night, introduce the "Television Show-Theme Charades" idea and explain the following rules:

Game rules

(1)   Each group member takes a turn pulling a television show's name out of the box/bag (or hat), and silently reads the name. That person then has to hum, sing, play (on a musical instrument), or whistle the theme song to the television show he or she selected.

(2)   If the person doing the singing/whistling/playing can get someone to guess correctly, he or she earns two points and the person who guessed earns one, and gets to go next.

(3)   If no one is able to name the song in a set amount of time (say, thirty seconds), the sheet of paper with the "unguessed" song goes back into the box/bag (or hat) and the person goes again. If that person draws the same show again, she or he gets another try until a new theme song is chosen.

(4)   *Extra points* can be earned for naming regular characters who appear on each program. When someone guesses a theme song correctly, that person gets to name a character on the show (it must be the name of a character, not the actor's actual name). Only one extra point can be earned per theme song.

(5)   Each time someone guesses incorrectly, she or he loses a point.

(6)   The person with the most points after all of the theme songs have been exhausted wins the game.

If there are controversies over any of the tunes, you can then scan through your tape and locate the tune in question. Also, after the Charades part of the evening is over, the group can take time to listen to all of the songs on the tape and discuss the shows or theme songs themselves.

Option #2
Traditional Charades rules

The above game can also be played according to traditional Charades rules if there are enough members present. In that format, it can be a stimulating game at parties or sleep-overs, when other families visit, during holidays, or at family functions.

Exercise #3
These songs are me!

Purpose: To learn about friends by getting to know their favorite music. To stimulate group play and social interaction.

Materials needed: Paper, pen/pencil, small box or bag.

Ages: Eight to twelve; four to ten children.

Step 1. The children are asked to write the titles of three songs that they feel somehow describe them on a small sheet of regular white notebook paper, fold it in half, and bring it to the party. As the children arrive they place the folded sheets of paper in the box or bag.

Step 2. When it is time for the game to begin, the children sit in a circle at the center of the party room. The party host begins the game by randomly selecting one of the folded lists and reading the song titles out loud. He or she gets first shot at guessing whose list it is.

Step 3. If the host is incorrect, the list goes back into the bag and the person at his or her right then randomly selects a list and has a try.

Step 4. Once someone is able to correctly identify an individual by his or her song list, that child may then begin to collect points.

Earning points
Points may be gathered in the following manner (either an adult or someone chosen by the group keeps track of the points):

(1) Being able to sing each entire song = ten points per song.

(2) Being able to sing at least one verse and the chorus = five points per song.

(3) Being able to sing any one part of the song = three points per song.

(4) Naming the artist = five points per song.

(5) Explaining what about each song describes the person whose list they selected, or how the song pertains to her or him = five points per song.

Step 5. Once a child has made a correct guess, and relates how the songs on the list describe his or her friend, the latter then gives feedback and adds any information that explains why she or he selected those particular songs. It is then that person's turn to go next and select the next folded sheet from the bag.

After every player has had a turn, the points are tallied, and the one with the most points wins.

Exercise #4
Can't judge a group (or an artist) by looking at the cover!

Purpose: To introduce children to their parents' music while also teaching that looks can be deceiving.

Materials needed: A stack of old, long-playing albums from parents' collection. (Tapes or CDs of parents' music will also work, although the cover art is much smaller and not as effective as the LPs!) Record, tape, or CD player and sound system.

Ages: Eight to twelve.

Step 1. Parent selects a number of LPs or CDs from his or her collection. Try to select groups the children will not be acquainted with. Try to present as much artist diversity as possible.

Step 2. Before songs are played the adult shows the children a cover and asks them what they think, based on the cover, the music will sound like. Each child takes a turn making guesses.

Step 3. Once the guessing is done, two or three songs from the record are played.

The players then discuss how much the music either did or did not reflect the look of the cover and their expectations.

Step 4. The parent can then use this opportunity to illustrate how looks can be deceiving, and how marketing plays a large part in selling music through carefully planned packaging. This can include such things as dressing up a group to fit a "clean" or "tough" image, making a cover very colorful or shocking, or using catchy titles or other advertising gimmicks.

Options

- While playing the music, have your children illustrate what type of dancing they think goes with the music.
- Depending on the children's level of shyness, have them also portray the performers by playing "air-guitar" or offering other musical mimicries.
- Use this opportunity to teach a thing or two about this particular artist (or group) and give your opinion as to why this artist did, or did not, "make it." Parents can also purchase books that summarize thousands of rock-era albums with group biographies, historical facts, and other interesting information they can pass on to their children.

Exercise #5
Noise Party!

Children like to make noise. They need to make noise. Making noise is one way of exploring, and discovering, sounds. As exasperating as it is to adults, banging a metal spoon against a tin can may sound like music to a one-year-old. Later, as the child matures, the instruments change but the sound of "heavy metal" continues to represent maddening music in many forms. Spoons become guitars, tin cans mutate into drum sets, food trays migrate into sound processors, and the piercing, shrieking voices find an ally in microphones and million-watt sound systems. In fact, given how much musical styles change across generations, the only constant seems to be the "parent irritation factor," an apparent prerequisite for each new generation's music. If it excites and stimulates the children, it will quite likely annoy and even enrage the parents. If it doesn't, then the present generation's music makers are not doing their job of creating intergenerational barriers and helping to kick-start the individuation process.

Purpose: To allow the children a forum for self-expression, where they may release pent-up energies and bond with peers.

Materials needed: See below.

Ages: All (parents should use discretion and keep younger children away from excessive noise).

The premise for a Noise Party! is very simple.

> Step 1. Get a group of children together in a safe, sound-insulated space, and give them permission to explore and express their need for clamorous fanfare.

> Step 2. Although instruments will help to get the party started, children can pretty effectively make noise without help from a lot of expensive equipment. A number of simple, safe instruments can help to contain the situation, providing focus and some sense of control (see below).

> Step 3. Having secured a safe space and provided the noisemakers, review the following game rules and let the Noise Party! begin.

Game rules
- Noise Parties! must be planned and supervised by parents.
- Time limits should be set. (Fifteen to twenty minutes is typically a long enough time to "just make noise!" At most, thirty minutes should be plenty of time to exorcise one's noise demons!)
- To assure safety, only the instruments (whether homemade or store-bought) provided and approved by adults should be used.
- Once the time limit is up, parents should—with the assistance of all children—collect all of the instruments, put them away and announce that the Noise section of the party is over.

· Noise Parties! should be followed by more sedate, quieting activities.

Percussion instruments, simple to play and noisy by nature, are a Noise Party's instruments of choice. Some of these include:

Suggested Noise Party! instruments:

Tambourines and whistles	Tambour
Floor tom-toms	Timbales
Assorted bells	Woodblock
Cymbals	Kettle and hand drums
Bongos and conga drums	Gongs
Cowbells	Rap sticks and blocks
Vibra slaps	Musical washboards
Jews' harps	Rattles, shakers and jingles
Calypso steel drums	

Many percussion instruments are available for physically challenged children and are usually assembled on specially built mounts so that they may be played with one, or even no, hands. A number of moderately priced, regular percussion instruments, such as the ones listed above, are also available in smaller sizes for children (see General Resources in Appendix B).

Other recommended instruments include:

Trumpets and other horns	Ocarinas and kazoos
Recorders	Glockenspiels
Metallophones	Xylophones
Guitars	Banjos
Harmonicas	Keyboards

Dijiri-tubes (a small version of the Didgeridoo)

Pennywhistles, bosuns, sirens, police, train, tug-boat, bird-sound, and any other assorted whistles

Sound resources recommended for nurturing your child with group activities

(Parents are also referred to Music Menu 16 in chapter 5 for a number of stimulating, energizing music titles and collections.)

Music Menu #23
Classic collections

If parents or their children like a particular artist or style, compilation packages or "Greatest Hits" collections are a good way to go for parties and other peer group activities. The following are particularly good collections from popular artists or labels.

Bert and Ernie's Greatest Hits	Sesame Street
The Baby's Gift of Music and Stories (box set)	Stories to Remember
Muppet Hits	The Muppets
Platinum: All-Time Favorites	Sesame Street
Barney's Favorites (box set)	Barney
The Bird Is the Word	Big Bird
Favorite Songs	Sesame Street
A Child's Celebration of Song	Various Original Artists
The Chipmunk Songbook	The Chipmunks
Danny Kaye for Children	Danny Kaye
The Dr. Seuss Collection (box set)	Dr. Seuss
Schoolhouse Rocks! (box set)	Schoolhouse Rock
Songs from the Aristocats	Aristocats
Bibbidi Bobbidi Bach (Disney songs)	Various Artists
101 Favorite Children's Songs (traditional tunes)	The Special Music Company
Playtime: 49 Favorite Action and Sing-Along Songs	CEMA Special Markets
For Our Children	Various Artists
For Our Children Too	Various Artists
All-Time Greatest Hits	Ray Stevens

Music Menu #24
Broadway musical show tunes

Annie	*Bye Bye Birdie*
Carousel	*Cats*
Finian's Rainbow	*Funny Face*
Guys and Dolls	*Oklahoma*
Porgy and Bess	*South Pacific*
The Music Man	

Music Menu #25
Fun/silly/goofy music

These CDs are also superb for car trips and parties.

A Child's Celebration of Silliest Songs	Various Artists
Camp Woof	Bill Wellington
Children's Favorite Silly Songs	Various Artists
Clowntown	Sphere Clown Band
Crock O'Christmas	Ren and Stimpy
Dancin' Magic	Joanie Bartels
Dinosaurs and Dragons	Kevin Roth
Disney Funny Food Songs	Various Artists
Disney Silly Songs	Various Artists
Funny 50's and Silly 60's	The ReBops
Hi Kids!	Shari Lewis
Krazy Songs	Kangaroo Kids
Kritter Songs	Kangaroo Kids

Mad Grooves: A Cheesy Collection of Old and New Mad Grooves

Mickey Unrapped	Various Artists
More Silly Songs	Disney
Naughty Songs for Boys and Girls	Barry Louis Polisar
Peanut Butter Jam	Various Artists
Radio Daze	Ren and Stimpy
Really Silly Songs About Animals	Bethie
Silly Songs	Sesame Street

Sillytime Magic	Joanie Bartels
Trout Fishing in America	My World
Very Silly Songs	Kidsongs
Very Silly Songs	Veggie Tales
Wacka Wacka Woo Other Stuff	Bill Harley

SOUND HUNTING: SOUND SAFARI

The purpose of the following activity is to provide a number of creative opportunities designed to enable parents and their children to spend quality time together while raising their collective sound awareness.

> *When we were kids my mom and dad came up with this game where we'd go out in the woods or by a lake, stand in a circle, close our eyes and hold hands. Dad would tell us to just "relax and listen with our ears open!" We'd stand there, for about five or six minutes, and just take in all the sounds that would happen to come by. It was absolutely amazing, and the funny thing was that we'd always hear new things and, after we'd leave, our hearing always seemed to be so much more acute. After those few minutes we'd open our eyes, sit down and share all the different sounds we'd "discovered."*
>
> —Kevin, nineteen, painter

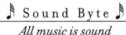

♪ Sound Byte ♪

*All music is sound
but all sound is not (necessarily) music.*

Purpose: To locate and collect random sounds.

What you need: Writing pad or notebook, pen or pencil, sense of adventure.

Optional: Small portable tape recorder with microphone.

Ages: Toddlers and older.

Tell your child, or children, that you are going on a "Sound Safari."

The primary idea is to be a "sound observer," or "sound listener," rather than a participant or "sound maker."

The "sound area" can be anywhere you can be, indoors, out, or both.

If you choose a yard or park in the fall, for instance, you may opt to forgo the well traveled routes and instead make your way through the colorful, crackling leaves that cushion the autumn landscape.

Be attentive to the sounds you make trampling over the crumbling twigs, fallen limbs, rustling leaves, shallow puddles, and any other "step-ables" that you happen upon along your path.

Be *sound aware*.

You may choose to log the more interesting sounds in your notebook or tape them on your recorder. If your child has not yet learned to write, he could perhaps handle the tape recording chores. If his writing skills are up to the task you may find it fun to alternate between being the "sound transcriber" (the person who writes the sounds down) and the "sound describer" (the person who describes what the sounds are "called").

Encourage your child to be inventive when describing the sounds, making up words that echo the random sounds as closely as possible.

Allow the sounds to dictate the words. Words like "crrackt," or "sloosh," for instance, may capture the spirit of actual sounds better than "real" words. Have fun with the sound descriptions. You may also choose to take votes as to how many "r's", "t's" or "p's" the spelling of the sound "should" have. Remember, the objective here is not formal transcription but rather raising sound awareness. Have fun!

You may choose to lie down on a blanket in your back yard and simply allow the sounds to rush or meander around you. Close your eyes, tilt your head, stare straight ahead, let your awareness reach far out into the distance, and tune in to the natural stereo effect that we so often take for granted. Make notes of the various sounds, discuss them, or simply allow them to come and go. Appreciate the nature of true "surround sound."

Can you hear the music in any of these sounds?

Select one particular sound and give it a chance. Listen to it for a while and see if you can begin to hear the music it is trying to play for you.

Listen to how other sounds create a natural harmony if you simply allow them to.

Listen for sounds you've "never heard" (or noticed) before. You will be surprised at how many sounds we take for granted. Let your imagination go wild. Do any of these sounds remind you of a song or an instrument you've heard before?

Do not allow "why's" to get in the way (e.g., "Why do crickets make that sound?" "Why do squirrels run all around in constant desperation?" "Why is it that we see jet planes before we can hear them?") If "why's" get in the way, return to your purpose: listening.

If your child is in the mood to be a bit more analytical, try focusing instead on:

What is making the sound?

How is it making it?

Where is the sound coming from?

When is it sounding?

Sometimes "why's" simply get in the way.

Listen to sounds within sounds . . . sounds around sounds . . . sound textures and combinations . . . harmonies, melodies, discordant sounds.

Note which are pleasant or unpleasant. What makes them pleasant or unpleasant?

If you are writing down the sound descriptions, be frugal: economize. Allow your "sound words" to be as simple as the sounds themselves. Words like "plunkt . . . kkkrrsh . . . floosh" are perfectly acceptable. Flow with the sounds and allow them to flow through you.

On a separate expedition, you may choose to record some of your sound experiences in a journal. Focus on the feelings and thoughts that the sounds bring out and stimulate.

If you choose to record the sounds, you will be able to return to them later. One idea is to play them back during a family function, a car trip, or a pajama party as you invent your own games of "name that sound!" If you do this, it is best to catalog them in the order that they are recorded, again, being brief but descriptive in your narration: "mockingbird," "dove," "neighbors' air blower," "rake against the sidewalk," "kitty playing in the leaves," "dripping kitchen faucet." That way, you will be able to identify them correctly as they are played back.

Or simply save them for a rainy day.

SOUND RESOURCES FOR NURTURING YOUR CHILD WITH ENVIRONMENTAL AWARENESS

Environmentally conscious tunes

Environmental Songs for Kids	Coco Kallis
Healthy Planet, Healthy People	The Van Manens
Evergreen, Everblue	Raffi
Earth Tunes	World Patrol Kids
Mother Earth	Tom Chapin
This Land Is Our Land: Yogi Bear Environmental Album	Yogi Bear and Friends

10

CREATING NURTURING SOUND ENVIRONMENTS

When designing a home's environment, most families consider a number of details and objects. Some of these include furniture style, drapes and curtains, paint or stain, wallpaper, rugs and carpets, ceiling lights and lamps, fans, plants, decorative objects, mirrors, and artwork. Few people, however, consciously consider music and sound as a preplanned, essential part of their atmospheric mosaic. The purpose of this chapter is to raise sound awareness of the fact that music helps to add a decorative "fourth dimension" to living, working, and recreational environments.

Most parents would not expect a twelve-year-old child to adjust his or her room's "vibrational ambience" by playing children's lullabies. Likewise, most parents would not typically play rap or heavy metal music to help set the mood as they relax in their own bedrooms. Music played in a child's room should echo the room's general feeling. For example, just as stuffed toys and pictures of happy, cuddly animals help to build and maintain a sense of harmony, the music played in a young child's room should echo these positive feelings of warmth and comfort. For infants and toddlers, children's music, music-box tunes and a lot of classical and New Age music selections provide many excellent choices that children will enjoy and benefit from (see Music Menus 14, "Music for Nurturing Children with Relaxation," and 23, "Classic Collections"). Preschoolers and school-age children, however, begin to branch out and state their preferences quite adamantly. As their vibrational makeup changes, growing children want their music to reflect their stage of development or personal identity.

Unable to control much of anything, music gives us something that can be controlled and modified according to our mood at the moment. Just as most parents want their children to try out different types of food, play with more than one friend, and study many subjects, music too is something that children need to experience in different forms.

The music that toddlers, preschoolers and school-age children are exposed to, however, should be monitored, approved, and supervised by parents. Just as the choices you make in other areas of life (foods you eat, clothes you wear, people you interact with, movies and programs you watch, places you vacation in) will help to shape your children's personal preferences, the music you introduce will help to encourage and animate their musical directions.

> *My recollections of my childhood bedroom are wonderful. I've always remembered a large room with warm colors and a feeling of comfort and safety. Vibrant prints adorned the walls and a horde of magnificent stuffed animals provided company in times of sorrow or joy. I always thought of it as the perfect room, far superior to any of my friends'. Recently, while sorting through some old photos I hadn't seen in years, I stumbled across some pictures of that room that Mom took on my eighth birthday. There I was, biggest smile you can imagine and not a care in the world. But the room itself, small, cramped, with lackluster colors and worn-out toys, seemed to betray every trace of those spectacular memories. I was so shocked that, at first, I didn't have the heart to say anything to Mom. Later, however, I felt compelled to mention how distorted my memories of that room had become over the years. Without hesitation, she quickly reminded me of the one thing missing from the pictures, the magical element that still echoed in my mind, making it all come alive. "That's because the music is missing from the pictures," she said, and I realized that, all along, it had been the vibrations of that wonderful music that continued to resonate those beautiful memories for me.*
>
> —Shelby, thirty-six, travel agent

MUSIC IN THE HOME: A TIME AND PLACE FOR EVERY TUNE

Music can have very powerful, or subtle, effects on the general mood one wants reverberating throughout one's home. Selective sounds and music, much like furniture and decorations, can easily be used in separate rooms to portray each family member's own personality while creating a desired ambience. Like everything, there is a time and a place for all (well, most) types of music. Used consciously, music can help to create and enliven the feelings, or vibrations, that we want to experience at different times throughout our homes. Rock or rap music regularly preferred by pre-teens and teenagers, for instance, is usually not a parent's top choice during supper or while relaxing over a cup of coffee and reading the morning paper.

One of the primary benefits that music affords is portability. In most homes, once a sofa is purchased and a particular artwork is hung over the fireplace, that "look," and the feelings it evokes, are pretty much set for a while. Sofas and armchairs can be repositioned and new decorations brought out to replace the old ones, but there are limits to how many different ways a living room can be physically rearranged and how much artwork most of us can afford. Even plants, portable and ever changing, are limited by space and the number of ways in which they can be pruned and arranged.

Music, on the other hand, can be changed almost instantly. In effect, music is an effective and fairly inexpensive tool that can be used to help set, and change, the feeling and "vibrational ambience" of a room depending on one's mood or particular needs at the moment. In addition, the rapid growth of miniature, moderately priced, high-quality sound systems over the past few years has made the possibility of portable, state-of-the-art musical environments more popular than ever.

Even if a sound system remains in one central location, the growing availability of diverse music styles gives us the option of modifying rooms by simply switching CDs or tapes. Over a twenty-four-hour period, for instance, different types of music can help to convert a family room from a space where Dad practices his morning yoga; to a relaxing haven where Mom and Dad read the morning paper and gather their thoughts for the day; to a babysitting nursery that caters to playtime, lunch, reading hour, naptime, then playtime once again; to Mom's after-work "gym"; to family-time room; to part-time home office where bills and other household matters are addressed before retiring for the day.

A moderately priced sound system, with speakers properly placed, can project music that will help a room feel larger, less cluttered, livelier, fresher, or simply more comfortable.

In selecting more specific types of music to help "set the mood" from room to room, a number of simple suggestions can be considered.

CREATING SOUND HOME ENVIRONMENTS

Music played when the entire family is together should effect a soothing, yet mildly stimulating ambience. This should be music mostly chosen by Mom and Dad, music they feel sets a mood of "refreshing calmness." Instrumental music is usually the best for creating this type of atmosphere. Baroque music, compilations of soothing classical music, and a lot of New Age music works very well for creating this ambience. On the other hand, a number of "nature" sounds, reproduced through sound generators (e.g., waterfall, rainforest, loons, and other bird sounds) serve as wonderful alternatives for creating pleasant sound environments. If the actual sound of gurgling, rolling water is what you prefer, a number of fairly inexpensive indoor water fountains are available through many catalogs and at some department or specialty stores.

> I grew up in a home where suppertime was the one time during the day when the entire family got together, and I always loved it. When Jim and I were starting our own family, that was one of our objectives, to make family meals an enduring tradition.
>
> It started out fine, but as the kids grew a little older it somehow started to unravel. One night, we decided that we needed a common theme, something extra that would entice the family to sit down together during meal times. We came up with the idea of "theme night," where each family member would choose a musical background that somehow reflected some aspect of the evening. Italian food, for example, called for composers or singers from that country, while Mexican food called for Latin music

of Mexican origin. Holidays were particularly fun and, while some—like Christmas, the Fourth of July, and Halloween—were easy, we would have a ball coming up with Easter, Thanksgiving, or Mother's Day music. We also found that it was a great way to introduce the kids to the purpose behind these holidays and educate them about different aspects of American history and traditions.

The topper, however, occurred during my husband's thirty-second birthday party. Our ten-year-old daughter Brooke actually went out and bought a CD compilation of songs that had been top hits in the year he was born. We now play that CD every year for his birthday and have gotten similar compilation discs for everyone else in the family.

—Laura, thirty-seven, office manager
for a financial corporation

The following sound musical ideas provide families with suggestions they can consider to help enhance sound vibrations at home.

MUSIC: THE FOURTH DIMENSION

Environmental home music should be given as much attention as other tools that help to create desirable, comfortable climates. Just as you would not want the air conditioning down too low, or the heat up too high, so too should musical selections and the volumes at which they are played be monitored and adjusted. Just as posters, toys, paintings, pictures, wallpaper, and decorations help to set the tone for an individual's room, music can add a "fourth dimensional" component that can help to personalize a room.

It's suppertime: dinner music
Dinner music should be relaxing and soothing. Music played as background to a family meal should be played softly so as to encourage, but not to interfere with, family conversations and discussion, as well as digestion! In other words, it should be as inconspicuous as the plants,

wallpaper or woodwork that enliven your dining room, while adding a sense of grounding and comfort.

Playtime

Playtime music in the family room should reflect the mood and purpose of the activity. Music played for a two-year-old child playing with blocks or assembling a puzzle can help to focus and relax the child. On the other hand, parents must keep the music at a low volume to assure that they can hear the child at all times.

Playtime also provides ample opportunities for parents to "sneak in" Big Band classics, ethnic lullabies, rock and pop music from the "golden era," traditional folk songs, world beat music, show tunes, and certainly the Baroque and classical music that is generally suggested for any number of activities. By acknowledging that children do not live in a social vacuum, and that, as they grow up, influences from friends, peers, and the media will become increasingly powerful, parents need to also be sound aware of their child's evolving needs and respectful of their evolving preferences and individuality.

Reading time

Music selected with sound awareness will help to enhance the benefits of particular activities for your children. Children engaged in reading, for example, often benefit from listening to music that helps to increase concentration, quiet the mind, stimulate alertness, and minimize external sounds that may otherwise be distracting.

A very popular musical option, and one typically found to be most universally effective for reading and concentration, includes largo movements from Baroque string concertos. More generally, however, hundreds of available compilations of classical and Baroque music available have been specifically designed to improve focusing and facilitate a learning response (see General Resources in Appendix B).

Activating the "artist within"

By setting a particularly active, yet relaxing tempo, the Baroque music mentioned above will also help to set a tone for cooperative play among children, while encouraging exploration and promoting a cheerful, positive climate.

Many children's activities, however, lend themselves to more active forms of music. Some forms of artwork, such as drawing, fingerpainting, sketching, and others that involve rhythmic movements, are often enhanced through stimulating, energetic music. For these purposes, moderately loud, animated music works well, as it tends to energize and invigorate children, activating their "artist within." By helping to release pent-up energies, and to arouse multiple sensations, music adds a "fourth dimension" as it complements other forms of artistic expression.

Soundtracks for the long and winding road

In their quest to become fully functioning individuals, children follow a path of exploration in which they are pioneers of their own destiny. Along this path they will have to make many choices. Some will be "good," others "bad," and others basically inconsequential. This is how we learn. All together, however, these journeys along the road of discovery provide experiences that will help to shape and mold your infant into a toddler, young child, teenager, and eventually, an adult.

The option of playing different types of music to help cushion your children's environment, be it the playroom, nursery area, bedroom, family room, or garage—if this is where they "hang out" and play—can also be an opportunity to introduce them to many types of musical influences in an unobtrusive way. Using your imagination and the suggestions given throughout this book as references, consider different types of music that can help to soothe or stimulate your child's environments.

ON THE ROAD AGAIN: MUSIC FOR FAMILIES ON THE MOVE

There are at least four major types of sound awareness—raising activities that we can engage in during car trips and long commutes:

(1) Listening for entertainment.
(2) Sing-alongs.
(3) Literacy—creating "road scholars."
(4) Hodgepodge: musical games for the road.

Overall, they are all intended to:

(a) Help time go by faster.
(b) Keep everyone alert and awake.
(c) Provide a good time.
(d) Motivate family bonding.

By providing a number of recreational musical activities and deas, this section is designed to help reduce the tension and boredom that can so often dampen family outings involving extensive road travel.

> *We were the only kids I knew who actually liked going places with our parents. They would turn on the radio, full blast, and we'd sing, and laugh, and have a ball. If someone happened to pull over next to us, or pass us by, we'd just keep singing, smile and wave. Sometimes they'd laugh, other times they would smile back, and other times they'd shake their heads and look at us like we were crazy. We didn't care. The only other time I ever felt like that was when I was a teenager in love.*
>
> —Haley, forty-two, optician

Listening for entertainment: family "travel tunes"

The two major "sound bytes" here are: (a) democracy (i.e., respecting and valuing other people's preferences and opinions), and (b) taking turns.

It is very likely that each family member will have his or her own musical preferences. It is also very likely that what Mom and Dad like will be a millennium away from what their children enjoy.

Regardless of how similar or different the family members' tastes may be, chances are that each member is usually going to prefer listening to his or her own tunes. One way to get around this is to set guidelines. In effect, there should be a list of what travel tunes are not acceptable.

The "unacceptable list." For instance, if Audrey simply cannot bear the sound of Michael Bolton (Mom's favorite singer), then he goes on the "unacceptable list." If Julian's favorite music is heavy metal but Mom and Dad feel that this type of music may be hazardous to their driving nerves, then this also goes on the "unacceptable" list, and Julian gets to listen to metal on his own time.

Family drive soundtracks, then, should be composed of music that may cross musical tastes and boundaries, but that will not irritate or create discord. Whether the tunes chosen are for relaxation or stimulation, they should be ones that can be enjoyed—to some extent—by all members of the family.

Rule number two. Family members listening to isolated tunes on their personal sound systems is fine in certain situations. Doing this on a regular basis, however, may have the result of creating barriers, distancing the family members. A second option is to take advantage of this time together and use music to help stimulate family bonding and conversation. With a little forethought and creativity everyone can use this valuable time to share aspects of themselves as they set the mood, and inspire conversation ideas, through mutually selected musical soundtracks.

"Listen, Honey, you can hear them grow!" By exposing themselves to musical diversity, parents may realize that a lot of the music their children listen to is reminiscent of tunes they themselves grew up with. Likewise, children hearing music from their parents' generation are often astounded by how derivative the music of their generation tends to be. In addition, parents will learn a lot about their children by tuning in to their ever-changing musical preferences. In essence, they will "hear them grow." Likewise, children listening to their parents'

music often discover aspects of their own personal and musical roots, and gain insight into their parents as people.

Sing-alongs

Car rides are excellent times to share favorite songs. Mom and Dad can introduce their children to some of their childhood songs, while the kids can acquaint their parents with songs they may be learning at school, or from some of their favorite television programs.

This is also a wonderful time to be democratic and share! Go around the car and have each family member select a song he or she wants to sing next. Another way is to draw straws, or pick names out of a paper bag to decide who chooses the next tune.

Car sing-alongs can also revolve around themes. Some of these might include:

· Particular musical eras, such as the 50s, 60s, 70s, 80s, or 90s (see "Top 100 Super-Great All-Time Car Sing-along Oldies"—Music Menu 30—in Appendix A).

· Pop groups from the 60s, 70s, 80s, or 90s (see "Pop Artists by the Decade"—Music Menu 29—in Appendix A).

· Nursery and children's songs (see Music Menus 2 through 27, and 31).

· Rounds, such as "Row Your Boat" (where family members can take turns).

· Holiday tunes (see Music Menu 27).

· American classics (see Music Menu 20).

· Traditional ethnic songs from your (or your ancestors') country of origin.

· Folk songs.

· Movie soundtracks.

· Broadway tunes (see Music Menu 24).

· Television show songs.

· Funny songs (see Music Menu 25).

· Original songs.

· Pot luck (whatever comes on the radio!).

- A variation on the sing-along is "Name That Tune!"—which can take a number of different forms (see next page).

Car sing-alongs can also take different forms:

(a) Singing a cappella (i.e., without any musical accompaniment).

(b) Singing to musical accompaniment provided by one or more of the family members.

(c) Singing along with a CD, tape, or the radio.

Literacy: creating "road scholars"

In addition to providing entertainment for all family members, car sing-alongs can provide a number of educational components. Most parents are familiar with "home-bound" schooling. "Vehicle-bound" education, however, is a relatively uncharted but potentially rich, fertile area.

Exercise #1
Musical trivia games

> Purchase one of many available trivia-type games that list different musical facts and tidbits. These may be used while traveling to help educate your children about musical instruments, composers throughout the ages, different musical eras, popular songs, humorous or interesting facts about songs and artists, and a host of other music-related topics. Suggestions include "MTV: The Game!" by Cardinal, and "Hanson Trivia Book" by Matt Netter.

Exercise #2
Name that tune

> Each family member takes a turn selecting some of his or her favorite tunes to be played. Keeping score adds a bit of excitement and stimulates competition. Additional twists to this game can be "Name that title," "Who's this artist?" "What year is this from?" "What was the name of this singer's original band?" "Where is this band from?" "Name that soundtrack," and any other variations you can muster. A very interest-

ing variation is to purchase one of many available tapes of old television shows.

Exercise #3
Listen and read

Select a composer, musical style, era, or anything else you want your children to learn about. Bring along a CD/tape and a complementary book, article, or CD booklet that discusses the music or composer whose music you are playing. While the music plays softly in the background, take turns reading passages that reveal interesting facts about the artist, musical time period, or the music itself.

Exercise #4
Learn that note

Similar to trivia games, a number of products are designed to help children learn about music notes, musical characteristics, etc. These come in various levels from beginner to advanced, and serve as either introductory or refresher courses for budding or practicing musicians. Suggestions include "Crazy 8ths" by TK Designs, and "Disney Family Fun Activity Book: A Music Primer" from Disney.

Exercise #5
Expanding vocabularies

Use the travel time as an opportunity to teach your toddler new words, nursery rhymes, or children's songs. Special CDs and tapes designed for these specific purposes are readily available (see Music Menus 3 through 7).

Exercise #6
Foreign languages

Go to the library and check out a tape or CD of foreign-language songs. Exposure to music from other countries, and tunes sung in foreign languages, will introduce diversified sounds while often helping to stimulate your child's interest in multilingual pursuits. If you're planning a vacation to a foreign country, this is also an excellent way to help your family become accustomed to new, exotic sounds (see "Music for Learning Foreign Languages," Music Menu 6, and "Multicultural Diversity," Music Menu 21).

Exercise #7
Cultivating the classics

Choose a classical composer and feature his or her music as a soundtrack to your drive as you take in the sights along your travel route. For an added dash of education, if the tape or CD includes liner notes, stop the music between selections and read about the piece you just heard or are about to play. In addition to using these opportunities to introduce your children to well-known masters, such as Mozart, Beethoven, Bach, and other male composers, this is a good time to extend their knowledge into the realm of great women composers. Some extraordinary but lesser-known women composers include Hildegard von Bingen, Barbara Strozzi, Clara Schumann, Ethel Smyth, Ruth Crawford Seeger, Nadia Boulanger, and Fanny Mendelssohn. Other more contemporary women composers include Pauline Oliveros, Joan Tower, Ellen T. Zwilich, Libby Larsen, and Thea Musgrave.

Exercise #8
Name that instrument

Play some musical numbers and ask your children to try to identify which instruments are being highlighted or featured in the solos.

Exercise #9
What's she singing about?

Bring along some message or concept songs and ask your children to interpret each song's intention or message. Make sure that any feedback you give is supportive, objective, and challenging in positive ways.

Exercise #10
Home-cooked music

Expose your children to their heritage by bringing along music that is reflective of their ancestry. This can include folk songs, traditional tunes, or music about particular regions of the country. For added schooling, you can complement the music with readings related to the music itself, the regions being portrayed, or both.

Exercise #11
Creating family harmony

A captive audience is ripe for learning about two-, three-, or four-voice harmony. Choose some of your, or your children's, favorite songs that feature good, simple harmonies. First, have your children listen to a song and focus on the singers' voices. Then rewind and have them listen to the same song while focusing on the way the singers are harmonizing. Toward the end of the song, have them try to mimic the various voices. Rewind again, and this time, try to harmonize through the entire song as if you were part of the group. For good examples of harmony in pop music, have your children listen to groups like the Everly Brothers, the Beach Boys, the Beatles, the Temptations, Boys II Men, or the Backstreet Boys.

Hodgepodge: musical games for the road

Exercise #1
Dance a 'toon

Have your toddler bring along her favorite toy or doll and have her put on a puppet show to selected tunes.

Exercise #2
And the cow goes...

Younger children love imitating animal sounds. Bring along a tape of your children's favorite songs and, as it plays, encourage them to sing along, imitating various animal voices such as cows, kitties, dogs, sheep, horses, etc.

Exercise #3
Rhythm ride

Play selected songs with good, upbeat rhythms and beats, and have each family member (except the driver, of course) join the rhythm section by hand clapping, lap tapping, cheek popping, lip babbling, finger snapping, etc.

Exercise #4
ABC'inging

Go through the alphabet and take turns naming songs, or artists, whose names begin with each letter.

Exercise #5
Goofing

Choose some favorite tunes. Either while they play in the background, or as you sing a cappella, take turns making up goofy words that fit into the melody lines. For some wonderful examples, listen to Weird Al Yankovic's recordings.

Exercise #6
Making the rounds

Before leaving home, make a list of several well-known rounds for the family to sing in the car. If possible, purchase or borrow from the library a book that provides lyrics to these songs.

Exercise #7
Moving compositions

Choose a word, idea, or topic and take turns developing a song with each family member coming up with rhyming lines. Assign one family member to write down the lyrics as these are created so that you may sing the entire song once it is completed. The song's melody can be either an original, or borrowed from a standard tune.

Exercise #8
A laugh a note

> Borrow, purchase, or check out of the library humorous music, and laugh all the way to your destination. Car rides are also good opportunities to listen to tapes of old radio comedy broadcasts.

Exercise #9
The listening list

> This one works best for older children who have fairly well-developed writing skills. Once you are well en route to your destination, roll down all of the car windows and ask that everyone remain completely silent for a set period of time (the amount of time will depend on your children's ages, with older children being able to remain quiet and attentive for longer periods). Each family member is to listen attentively to every sound in the moving environment and make a list of the different sounds (train, wind, road bumps, car horn, rain on car roof). After the time limit is up, take a few minutes to discuss your sound observations. Rewind your minds and start again.

Exercise #10
One-quarter rest

> On especially long rides, bring along some soothing music, blankets, and pillows, and tell your children that this is their resting . . . relaxing . . . re-energizing . . . or meditating time. Everyone benefits.

Music Menu #26
Travel tunes

Baby Songs, Car Songs	Hap Palmer
Good Ship Lollipop	The Persuasions
Smart Music! Cartime	Smart Music!
Wee Sing in the Car	Wee Sing
Travel Tunes & Play Pack	Ronald McDonald

Ten Tunes to Go	Songs From the Back Seat
Beep Beep & Splish Splash	Joanie Bartels
Cars, Boats, Trains & Other Things that Go	Kidsongs
Disney Travel Songs	Various Artists
Classic Disney: Vols. 1 and 2	Various Artists
Sing-along Travel Songs	Sesame Street
Travelin' Magic	Joanie Bartels
Travel Songs	Disney
Car Songs	Kimbo Educational
Cars, Trucks and Trains	Kimbo Educational
Family Travel Classics: Billboard Presents	Various Artists
Toddlers Sing Playtime	Toddlers Sing Series

MUSIC AND HOLIDAYS: USING MUSIC TO GET IN TUNE FOR THE HOLIDAYS

Music and holidays fit together like hand and glove. At Christmas time, like it or not, the marriage is inescapable. Turn on the television and a great number of advertisements and commercials are saturated with holiday themes, and supported by holiday-type music. In many areas, grocery and department stores, malls, and even airports begin piping in Christmas music as early as October. Music has acquired the role of marketing "cue" to remind the children that the holidays are right around the corner and it's time for them to get their Christmas lists in.

What do I most love about holidays? The music! To me, music is like a family member we can always count on, like comic strip characters who never age. The same traditional songs that brought our family together when I was a kid are there for our growing family now, the same melodies and memories, as dependable as ever. Although everything else seems to change from year to year, "Jingle Bells," "O Come All Ye Faithful," and "White Christmas" forever remain the same. Listening to our two kids harmonizing to the same tunes we used to sing when we were their age is the highlight of our holiday season.

—Connor, thirty, father of two, court clerk

Holiday musical traditions

For many families, holiday music is the very essence of tradition: a renewing of energy and spiritual vibrations, a tapestry of hope and unity, a source of religious affirmations. On the other hand, while Jewish children celebrate Chanukah to tunes such as "My Dreydl," "O Hanukah," and "Light One Candle," and Christian children celebrate Christmas to the sounds of "Jingle Bells," "Rudolph the Red-Nosed Reindeer," and "Twelve Days of Christmas," they all learn early on to associate these melodies with holiday gifts and time off from school.

These songs, then, take on many meanings that extend beyond their religious and spiritual connotations. Children learn to associate holiday tunes with family travels, get-togethers, and other customs and traditions.

Holiday music can be a double-edged sword. Depending on a particular family's financial or emotional situation, holiday music can come to take on associations that add to existing feelings of joy or sadness, hope or pessimism, dread or delight. It can make the good better and the bad worse.

For struggling families with young children, holiday music can trigger issues that may be particularly difficult to work through. The "holiday spirit," supported by a vast universe of musical soundtracks, can add to escalating expectations, creating stress for parents and children alike—or it can revive memories of earlier, difficult holidays. During the holidays, everything seems to become magnified, and just as it does in the movies, television sitcoms, and advertising, music serves as a soundtrack—a cue—that can quickly and easily return us to those moments in time.

On the positive side, however, music is also the glorious soundtrack that returns us to moments of great fun and joy. There are many ways through which we can choose to take advantage of holiday time. Although we may not be able to control the music soundtracks when we venture out into the world during the holidays, we can often take control of what memories we choose to create during these particularly emotional periods.

Musical ideas for the holidays

(1)   Introduce your children to volunteer work. Volunteer your time, energy, and talents to a community organization, church or temple, nursing home, homeless shelter, or other place where you and your children may help others. During holidays, many of these sites welcome caroling troubadours and storytellers, or simple visits from children's groups that can help to renew spirits via sing-alongs or other musical activities. These acts of altruism often circle around back to us, bringing a sense of pride, and creating positive self-esteem and loving memories.

(2)   Be around others whom you enjoy. Music helps to make people feel closer. It promotes expression of thoughts and feelings and can help to stimulate feelings of either relaxation or activity. By helping to anchor, and later activate, memories, music helps us and our families to enjoy and later recall many good times as we add new memories to life's changing soundtracks.

(3)   The "you know it's coming" advantage. If you know from experience that a particular holiday time might trigger feelings of loneliness, sadness, or remorse, make plans ahead of time to seek alternatives to help improve your situation, emotionally and physically. Call on family or friends (someone supportive and with whom you will feel comfortable). Take advantage of the holiday. Begin new customs or traditions that will help to create new, positive associations. Join a support group or begin sessions with a therapist before the season arrives. How you handle the holidays will in turn affect how your children are affected by them.

(4)   Create your own soundtracks. In other words, if holiday music affects you in a negative way, play music of your own choice during the holidays. Use music as an ally to gain control of your environment. Don't let the environment control you. By doing this, we can teach our children to maximize their resources and raise awareness to things that we can control, rather than struggling with things that we cannot.

(5)   Begin an exercise program well before the season hits. Take advantage of music's motivational and stimulating effects, and

its ability to set the pace for different exercise rhythms. Regular exercise will help you to feel better and more confident about yourself. This will help to create vibrations that will undoubtedly be passed on to your children during particularly stressful times.

(6) Don't forget—to quote from a particularly popular title from the Big Band era—music can help to put us "In the Mood."

Music Menu #27
Music for the holidays

A Children's Chanukah	Various Artists
A Chipmunk Christmas	The Chipmunks
Arthur's April Fool	Marc Brown
Arthur's Halloween	Marc Brown
Be My Valentine	Richard Scarry
Christmas with the Chipmunks (Vols. 1 and 2)	The Chipmunks
Easter Egg Mornin'	Bobby Goldsboro
Halloween Fun	Kimbo Educational
Halloween Howls	Andrew Gold
Have Yourself a Looney Tunes Christmas	Various Artists
Holiday Songs for All Occasions	Kimbo Educational
Spooky Favorites	Favorites Series
Jewish Holiday Songs for Children	Rachel Buchman
Let's Celebrate Hanukah!	Elissa Oppenheim-Schreiner
Let's Celebrate Passover	Elissa Oppenheim-Schreiner
Mostly Ghostly Stories	David Holt
Sounds of Halloween	Various Artists
Spooky Tales & Scary Sounds	Various Artists
The First Easter Egg Ever	Richard Scarry
The First Halloween Ever	Richard Scarry
Franklin's Halloween	Franklin

11

WITH A LITTLE HELP FROM MY KIDS
It's Chore Time!

In today's busy world, parents—especially single parents—need as much family help and cooperation as possible in order to maintain clean and tidy households. Parents need to take responsibility for assigning, monitoring, and teaching age-appropriate chores, and to be firm and consistent in their expectations that their children will take part in these day-to-day family duties. The purpose of this chapter is to introduce ways through which daily chores and responsibilities can become enjoyable opportunities, where all family members can collaborate on ideas and contribute personal talents.

> *When I was a young girl, Saturday morning was the time for cleaning, vacuuming, dusting, and all of those weekly household chores. Every Saturday, Mom would play all the Motown stars— the Temptations, Smokey, the Supremes—to get us motivated and set the pace. I loved it. We had a blast and always looked forward to Saturday mornings because of the way she approached the whole thing. In my mind, it was like being in a musical where we got to be the stars! Now, with my kids, I'm continuing the tradition. In the meantime, it gives me a chance to hear what they're listening to, because my rule is that we all take turns choosing and playing whatever music we like. While they've introduced me to The Spice Girls, The Backstreet Boys, and Hanson, I've taught them about David Ruffin, Marvin Gaye, and Otis Redding. So, although some of the music has changed, the vibes are still the same.*
> —Erin, forty-two, gynecologist

Divvying up household duties is an excellent way for parents to spend time with their children and teach them a sense of sharing, collective effort, and personal responsibility. As many experienced parents know, however, motivation, physical ability, and maturity levels can fluctuate quite drastically among individual children, regardless of their ages. As a result, a child's age is only one factor parents should consider when determining what to expect from their children. In general, however, there are some broad, basic guidelines that parents may consider before assigning or entrusting household responsibilities to their children. They are offered here to provide parents with a general idea of what they may expect from children ages two to twelve.

AGE-APPROPRIATE CHORES: ONE YEAR AT A TIME

Two-year-olds. As early as age two, children can be encouraged and expected to learn about general cleanliness and neatness. When play-time is over, parents should always encourage the two-year-old tod-dler to be actively involved in putting the toys away.

Three-year-olds. By the time children reach their third year, parents can expect that, with help, their toddlers will begin to learn the process of organizing their toys in their proper places, rather than having them scattered messily throughout the house twenty-four hours a day. By age three, with guidance, toddlers are also ready to start becoming more personally invested in wiping their dirty faces, brushing their teeth, and even bathing and dressing themselves. This is also a good age to begin teaching order and organization.

Four-year-olds. With assistance, four-year-olds are typically capable of gathering and putting away their toys and games, picking up their clothes and placing dirty ones in the hamper, hanging up clean cloth-ing, and even making their beds. Many can begin fixing simple snacks and setting the table, as well as—again, with help from a parent or sib-ling—choosing their outfits and dressing themselves.

Five-year-olds. As emphasized above, up to about age five, most chil-dren will need a moderate amount of hands-on help to learn and carry through with their chores. By five, however, while some children begin to show signs of doing some tasks with minimal help, most—if not all—will need a great deal of supervision and/or reminding. At this age, many children can begin helping with the dusting, vacuuming, taking out the trash, looking after pets, helping Mom and Dad clear the table after dinner, and maintaining a cleaner, neater bedroom and playroom environment.

Six-year-olds. By school age, or around the age of six, children should be able—albeit with well-placed "hints" and guidance—to fix their own snacks, dress themselves, and become increasingly more aware of personal grooming.

Seven-year-olds. Well supervised and prompted, seven-year-olds are able to bathe and clean up after themselves (although shower or bath time may tend to fall at either "too short" or "too long" extremes). Hanging clothes and caring for the new kitty or puppy, although still an ordeal, will be within their range of capability.

Eight- and nine-year-olds. Eight- and nine-year olds are a better bet for helping to set and clean the dinner table, dressing, grooming, and picking up after themselves; they can even cook themselves simple, basic meals. Keeping their beds and playrooms clean and tidy may still take a bit of parental effort, but the basic tools should, by now, be all in place.

Ten- and eleven-year-olds. By the time children are ten or eleven, a lot of chores that once needed almost constant urging and adult management should begin to fall into place. Astonished parents will finally begin to see the fruit of their years of labor, prompting, and persistence budding right before their very eyes.

Twelve-year-olds. By twelve, most children should be expected to dress and groom themselves, keep clean and orderly rooms, help with the laundry, care for pets, take out the trash, and assist with other basic household tasks and duties. Assignments should now be carried out with little or no supervision as part of your child's regular routine.

Regardless of their children's ages, parents can assist them in understanding, remembering, and fulfilling their housekeeping responsibilities by raising their sound awareness. Following are a number of sound ideas for tuning up your household "vibes."

Sound Idea #1

Be there and be involved

During the first few years of doing chores, your child will need you there with the "three crucial M's:"

- Modeling,
- Motivating, and
- Mopping up (what does not get done).

Sound Idea #2

How does your "title" make you sound?

As you model for and train your child, it sometimes helps to think of yourself as an "advisor" or "consultant" (versus "the boss") who is giving suggestions (rather than orders), and overseeing or chaperoning (not dictating) the operation. Be a firm but gentle, active participant.

Sound Idea #3

Even great conductors need an orchestra

Remind your children that they are, indeed, valuable, irreplaceable, worthy members of the family unit. Use humor and straightforward language. Listen to what you say and hear how you say it.

Sound Idea #4

Create positive vibrations

Give praise at every opportunity. Recognize attempts and appreciate efforts. Compliments and commendations should not be limited to parent-child interactions, but should begin, and endure, at the parent-parent level. Acknowledging a job well done and showing mutual appreciation should be modeled whenever appropriate or relevant.

Sound Idea #5
Give sound advice

Avoid criticism, negativity, and sarcasm. Think instead of emphasizing structure, rewards, and positive, proactive ways to teach desired behaviors—such as through token systems, charts, and contracting. Where there are problems, propose solutions, options and alternatives. (See General Resources in Appendix B for books that specialize in the above behavioral approaches.)

JINGLES ALL THE WAY: TAKING ADVANTAGE OF THE MUSIC THAT'S THERE

What's your favorite commercial? For most of us born in the second half of the twentieth century, television has been a significant influence. From the very beginning, dramas, sitcoms, beauty pageants, news shows, documentaries, sports, and movies, regardless of their scope and diversity, have all shared one common feature: commercials. Over the years, television commercials have become so engaging and ingenious that at times they are actually more entertaining than the programs they sponsor. Advertising has been a consistent force in television, and even in this age of computer-enhanced digital wizardry it has held fast to a universal constant: music.

The music used to embellish commercials, and to sell and promote products, is chosen and programmed very carefully to appeal to specific target audiences. Commercials aimed at teenagers, for instance, move along to soundtracks that try to capture the spirit and rhythms of the adolescent culture. Likewise, products aimed at middle-aged parents try to appeal to the beat of their generation. A vast number of commercials for adults in the nineties were anchored by popular songs from the sixties and seventies, because this music served as the basic soundtrack for the baby-boom generation. In the same manner, children tend to learn and recall tunes and ditties that accompany children's commercials more easily than the suggestions and responsibilities that parents try to provide.

Below are a number of ways through which music can be used to assist parents in raising their children's sound awareness to household chores, personal responsibilities, and safety precautions. The following exercises are designed to help parents harness the power of music used in jingles and commercials to benefit their children. Before you move into the exercises, however, you need to work together with your children and decide which of their favorite jingles will be most appropriate to use for these activities.

Step 1. Ask your child to sing or tell you three or four of her favorite commercial jingles. If there are only one or two, then start with those; others will likely surface soon. As a starter, even one simple catchy melody will suffice for a while. Once you introduce this musical concept, your child will likely begin to pay closer attention to which jingles she finds most appealing. If nothing comes to mind right away, give her a couple of days, and keep reminding her to be attentive to commercial jingles as she watches her favorite programs.

Step 2. Have your child teach you the jingles (whether you already know them or not, this is a wonderful way to let children know that teaching can be mutual and that you respect their knowledge).

Step 3. Pen and paper in hand, sit together and go over the duties your child is responsible for. Although she may not have yet learned to read, the process of writing these duties down as you discuss them will help to plant the seeds of the purpose and importance of writing.

Food for the Ears

To further encourage interest in writing, reading, and coordinating efforts, read each duty aloud after you write it down, guiding your finger over the words and involving your child in the process.

Exercise #1
Creating personal musical messages

Step 1. Using the melody of one of your child's favorite jingles, sit down together and try to compose a new set of lyrics with words and rhymes that will serve as a reminder for chores and responsibilities (see next page for examples).

Step 2. Keep these short and simple, and try, as best you can, to fit them into the beat and melody of the commercial tune. This will make it easier to memorize and recall.

Step 3. A commercial jingle that is being played to the point of nausea today will most likely be history in a month or two. However, this gives you just about the right amount of time to use it to teach the rules and ideas that your rapidly changing and developing child needs to learn now!

Step 4. The fact that commercial jingles are representative of the here and now makes them a very good tool to use. As your child matures and new jingles surface, you will be able to draw from each new batch to help impart the new information your child needs.

The following limericks and melodies can serve as examples. Since, as stated above, popular commercials are broadcast for very short periods of time, the melodies I suggest as examples are based on popular tunes and melodies.

Musical examples
Tooth brushing (sung to the tune of "Here We Go Loopy Lou")
It's time to brush my teeth,
It'll take a little while,
Softly up, softly down,
And look at that beautiful smile!

Making the bed (sung to the tune of "Pop! Goes the Weasel")
I'm making up my bed today,
So early in the morning,
I fluff the pillows, tuck the sheets,
On, goes the morning!

Putting toys away (sung to the tune of "Camptown Races")
Putting all my toys away,
This one, that one,
Putting all my toys away,
Got plenty to do today!
It's no big deal at all, that's where they're gonna stay,

Putting all my toys away,
Then I go on my way!

Getting dressed (sung to the tune of "The Hokey Pokey")
I slip my right arm in, I slide my left arm through,
Then I button my shirt, every button through and through,
There is nothing to it, this is something I can do,
Just like the grownups do!
I slip my right leg in, I slide my left leg through,
Then I pull up my pants (jeans, shorts) and I do the zipper too,
There is nothing to it, this is something I can do,
Just like the grownups do!
I pull my right sock on, my left one makes a match,
So I put the left one on, I don't even have to watch,
There is nothing to it, this is something I can do,
Just like the grownups do!
(same as above, with "shoes")

Although this exercise may be difficult at first, with practice it will become easier. One of the advantages of creating one's own musical messages is that coming up with something original is immensely helpful in our being able to memorize and integrate the messages. Once done, the beat and the melody of the music will do the rest.

Because of music's great powers of association, from this point on, each time your children hear the jingle, be it on television or in their own minds, they will be immediately reminded of their personal musical messages.

Exercise #2
Safety dances

Just as music can be used to teach your toddlers and preschoolers a number of household responsibilities, the same tunes can be modified or used for teaching rules of thumb. The basic, universal reminders of safety and growing independence will become more pleasantly and readily ingrained by your children.

Musical examples

Street crossing (sung to the melody of "Twinkle, Twinkle Little Star")
Looking left and looking right,
Wait till there're no cars in sight,
Looking left and right again,
Wait till there're no cars and then,
Looking left and looking right,
I can cross and be all right!

Turning off appliances (sung to the tune of "I'm a Little Teapot")
Whenever I'm done I always know,
Turn things off before I go!

IT'S CLEAN-UP TIME!

Although harnessing the power of commercial jingles can be quite practical and effective, with a little patience, practice, and creativity, parents can use many different types of music and sound to help teach their children a number of diverse skills, including focusing, pacing, and personal responsibility.

In fact, any number of popular or traditional songs, nursery rhymes, or other tunes can—of course—be used very effectively for fulfilling the same purpose, and distilling the same information, as commercial ditties. As you are exploring this technique, you will quickly find that many of the tunes your child associates with a particular product due to its association with a recent television commercial are based on songs that may have been among your favorites back when you were toddling around.

To summarize, using music that your children can learn to associate with particular tasks will provide a number of benefits.

· Music is very helpful in helping children focus on the task at hand.
· It helps to set and maintain a tempo that guides a child's work speed.
· It helps to block out competing thoughts such as, "I want to go outside and play."
· It helps to add enjoyment to the chore, making it seem more like a game.

- It helps to give the children a timeframe for getting the room cleaned, or the chore done. For instance, if you estimate that a task will take your child fifteen minutes, select a number of songs or music that will play for that length of time. This can easily be done by programming a disc player, or making a special tape with songs totaling the desired time.
- It makes time seem to go by more quickly.

12

TAKING CARE OF YOURSELF
The Ultimate Investment

Raising children is one of the most challenging tasks adults can undertake. For single parents, and those with part- or full-time jobs, the time limitations posed by job responsibilities and the energy expended at work can take a significant toll. Many parents rush home after work to take care of seemingly endless responsibilities, such as laundry, grocery shopping, cooking and cleaning, and paying bills. In the end, something has to give. By the time they are able to take care of the tasks that "must" get done before the end of the day, they are in great need of a breather, and some alone time. When they are finally able to sit down for some quality time with their children, they often find that it is almost time for bed.

> *The memories I have of my dad are like this: By the time my brother and I got up for school in the morning, he had already left for work. Come nighttime, he would, at times, make it home early enough to tuck us in, usually just as we were drifting off to sleep. I guess the things I remember the most are his smell, and the sound of his voice, which was deep and comforting. On the weekends he worked a second job and again was up and gone well before we were up, and didn't get home until after we were already in bed. For a long time, I greatly resented Dad for not "being there" for us. Now with two boys of my own, I understand that his absence was necessary for him to be able to pay the bills, and to keep a roof over our heads. Thanks to him and his hard work, I was able to earn a degree, which has made it possible for me to work reasonable hours, and spend time with my own family. Thanks to him, I am a responsible adult who understands the meaning of sacrifice and hard work, and the pleasure and luxury of being able to be with my family. Thanks to him, I get to be myself.*
>
> —Justin, forty-eight, industrial engineer

Below are a number of sound suggestions to assist parents in taking care of themselves, so that they may maintain the healthy balance of mental, emotional, and physical resources that are necessary in caring for their children.

PREVENTION: A MINUTE OF LISTENING IS WORTH AN HOUR OF EXPLANATIONS

As best as possible, try to acquaint yourself with what you may generally expect throughout the various stages of child development. Chapters 2 ("Music and Language Acquisition"), 6 ("Sleepy-Time"), and 11 ("With a Little Help from My Kids") provide some age-related guidelines that parents can draw from to help set their expectations in particular areas. For additional insight into developmental stages, there are many excellent books available that outline and review these theories and principles in great detail and from different perspectives (see General Resources, in Appendix B).

PHYSICAL WELL-BEING

Strive to be of sound body and mind. A well-balanced, nutritional diet is necessary to fuel the body. Just as laptop computers, cellular phones, and other appliances need to be recharged, the human body needs energy so that it can continue to function effectively. Physical exercise, as discussed in earlier sections of this book, is essential for both children and adults to help keep us alert, vibrant, and in shape for life's demands.

REGULAR TUNE-UPS

Many of us neglect, or excuse away, the need for annual checkups of our most important machines: our bodies. If there is a history of specific medical problems in your family, take the time to make sure that you receive proper preventive care from your family physician. Annual medical checkups are a sound investment of both your time and money.

RELAXATION

Surprisingly, many adults work harder at not relaxing than at relaxing. Because of daily stresses, ambition, fear of failure, and other reasons, an astonishing number of adults seem to feel that relaxation equals laziness, or that it takes up time otherwise spent on being productive or accomplishing "more important things." Over the years, I have conducted many stress-management workshops. Once in a while, particularly when these are scheduled as part of a company's requirements, some participants will "go along with," or "endure" the stress management exercises, "tolerating" the torturous minutes of deep breathing and body scanning as they sit rigidly, arms tightly folded and teeth firmly clenched. When I've approached some of these individuals afterward, they often reveal that they find it very difficult to "give up control," or feel that relaxation "doesn't really work," or "is a waste of time." By denying themselves the luxury of the experience, they continue to live stressful, tension-filled personal and professional lives.

Relaxation is just as important for adults as it is for children. By taking time out for relaxation on a regular basis, parents can "recharge their batteries," clearing the way for body and mind to respond with renewed vigor and sound awareness. Parents are referred to chapter 4, "Sound Relaxation," for a quick review, or to one of the many excellent books on stress management (see General Resources, in Appendix B).

JUST GIVE ME TWENTY MINUTES...!

Parents are—by definition—very busy people who find it very difficult (if not impossible) to "carve out" twenty to thirty minutes each day to listen to a relaxation sequence on stereo headphones or to engage in meditation. From a sound awareness perspective, however, there are a number of other ways to ease up throughout the day, take breathers and find repose while going about our regular activities. The following ten sound suggestions offer some ideas.

Sound Suggestion #1
Pace yourself

Whenever you find yourself rushing to get something accomplished five minutes sooner, or to arrive home five minutes earlier, use that as a signal to slow down! Prioritize; there's no way of getting sixty-five seconds out of a minute, or twenty-five hours out of a day. Think of how much farther armies can march, birds can fly, and marathon runners can run simply by pacing themselves.

♪ Sound Byte ♪
Before turning on your sound system,
or speaking to your children,
always remember to adjust the volume.

Sound Suggestion #2
Breathe . . . breathe in the air . . .

Regardless of what we may be doing, we can usually work breathing in. The trick is to breathe consciously and raise our sound awareness to using breathing as a tool for relaxation. When you feel tense, anxious, or otherwise stressed and frustrated, use that as a signal to practice some sound breathing (i.e., breathing with full awareness that you are breathing for the purpose of calming down; listening to and feeling the breath as it enters, replenishes, then exits your body). Time spent in lengthy business meetings, sitting at traffic lights, and waiting in line at grocery stores provides excellent opportunities for sound breathing. Other excellent opportunities include:

· Whenever your children make you angry.
· Before you react to annoying or irritating situations.
· At the moment you feel you are about to make a sudden irrational decision.
· As you sense you are about to lose control of a situation.

Parents are again referred to the deep-breathing exercises in chapter 4 for some basic guidelines.

Sound Suggestion #3

Adjust your rhythms

Find pleasure in the rhythms around you, and—whenever possible—adjust your surrounding sound environment (e.g., with pleasant music or soothing sounds) so that the rhythms that surround you in turn help to slow you down and get you "in sync" with the world. Accept your limitations; think "flowing" versus "stumbling." As we get a little older, we begin to realize that some of the tasks we could do in our teens or twenties with little effort, start to become more strenuous and demanding.

Sound Suggestion #4

Sleep: Don't just lie there!

Many people feel completely alert, refreshed, and replenished after four or five hours of sleep; others need eight or nine. By adjusting your daily rhythms, and listening to the messages from your body and mind, you can make getting a good night's sleep a priority among your daily routines. Parents are encouraged to review some of the sound suggestions shared throughout the Sleepy-Time chapter (chapter 6) to help them with their own sleeping patterns.

Sound Suggestion #5

Self-messages

Listen to any messages that you give to yourself that tend to make you tense, anxious, and stressed. Counter these with thought-stopping techniques, focusing on positive attributes of yourself or the situation, or try putting stress-provoking issues in perspective. Treat yourself to positive, adaptive, and encouraging affirmations. Remind yourself of your good qualities, that your children need you, and that you need yourself. Empower and nurture yourself by focusing on your ability to grow and change, and exercise your right to move forward (or around situations) as you learn from life's opportunities and challenges (again, see General Resources, in Appendix B, for books on stress reduction).

Sound Suggestion #6

Thank you for being a friend

One of the best things about friends is that we get to choose them. Friendships, like children, require cultivation. Surround yourself with supportive, positive vibrations. Good friendships (including those with family members) are a two-way street. Sometimes when we're down we need a friend to help pull us up. Other times, when we are feeling up, we may need to help a friend through a bad period. One of life's secrets is achieving the proper balance.

Sound Suggestion #7

Listen to others

Quite often our stress comes from not tuning in to what others are saying, which results in our making avoidable mistakes, or worrying unnecessarily about what the message really meant. By listening attentively to others, and tuning in to our responses, we can more carefully maintain a better balance between our needs and our commitments to others.

Sound Suggestion #8

Use "negative vibration blocking"

The ability to tune out negative messages is just as important as the skill of listening to others. When others share particular bits of "wisdom" that you find upsetting to your ways of thinking, or that cause undue stress or confusion, either put them in perspective or let them go. Exercise your right to set limits when faced with demanding phone calls from friends or relatives who may tend to use you as a "sound board" for random, personal problems. Remain sound aware to your needs versus theirs, and utilize your option to distance yourself from falling into the stressful role of therapist or caretaker.

Sound Suggestion #9

Alone time: alone again . . . unnaturally

Just as we need friends, we also need ourselves. Once again, however, as with relaxation, some adults have difficulty separating "being alone" from "being lonely." As a result, they try to fill every minute with activities or commitments that keep them in touch with others. Later, drained from trying to meet exhausting demands, they find themselves complaining that they don't have "time for themselves."

At some time during your day, take some time to be alone with yourself. Take twenty minutes to strap on a portable sound system and go for a walk, engage in some stress-reduction exercise, or pursue a pleasurable activity, be it gardening, watching the sunset, or walking around a lake. By spending time with yourself, you will open up the personal space you need to allow others back in.

Sound Suggestion #10
Professional help: If you speak, they will listen

If you feel that the issues you are facing are insurmountable, out of the ordinary, or simply beyond your potential grasp at the moment, do not hesitate to seek professional help. Many people are pleasantly surprised to find how much better they feel after meeting with a psychologist, counselor, or clergyperson who can help to offer support, viable alternatives to particular situations, or simply an objective ear. Just as you would seek assistance from a physician for a sprained ankle, do not hesitate to consult a spiritual or mental-health professional when dealing with situations affecting your emotional, psychological, or spiritual well-being.

AND, IN THE END...

By taking care of themselves, parents are sending a message to their children that this process is an invaluable, fundamental aspect of life. By role-modeling self-nurturing behaviors, thoughts, and attitudes, parents are helping to raise sound awareness that will establish the vibrations for happy hearts, smart minds, and confident souls.

ENCORE! GROWING CHILDREN

In a lot of ways, having and raising children is like starting and caring for a flower garden. You set the foundation to the best of your ability, and select the right spot in the yard where the flower will receive just the right amount of sunshine, but still be protected from the elements. You plant the seed, carefully nurture it, and hope that a beautiful, healthy flower develops. Once the flower arrives, you admire it, tend to it, and nourish it with love, support, and nutrition, pruning and weeding as necessary, and protecting it from cold and from insects and predators. All the while, however, you realize that there is a limit to how much you can do, and that the flower has to follow its path and develop according to its own natural plan. It all comes down to giving of yourself, unconditionally, and knowing when to let go. In the end, the flower is its own reward.

—Rachel, twenty-six, cosmetologist

Children are the flowers in your family garden. Nurture them by providing plenty of sunshine, nourishment, love, and tenderness, and give them plenty of room to grow.

In planting the seeds, always remember to weed out:	*And, in their place, sow and reap:*
Guilt	Understanding
Blame	Praise and encouragement
Hopelessness	Hope
Shame	Respect
Neglect	Nurturing
Rejection	Acceptance
Anger	Patience
Worry	Confidence

Distrust	Trust
Insecurity	Grounding
Dependency	Self-reliance
Panic	Calm and centering
Perfectionism	Humanness
Negativity	Positivity

In essence, when you speak your words of wisdom, think of where they're headed—listen to what you say, and how you say it.

APPENDIX A

ADDITIONAL MUSIC MENUS

Music Menu #28
Quick glossary of popular music styles

Alternative
Many people misunderstand "Alternative" music to mean tunes composed of hard and irritating sounds. In actuality, the term "alternative" stands for just about anything that is an "alternative" to mainstream rock and pop. A lot of Alternative music is very melodic, soothing, and pleasant, and supported by positive, uplifting lyrics and melodies. As in any case, increase your sound awareness before you buy.

Ambient
Aptly described by one of my regular child clients as "floating music," Ambient music is essentially music to "relax and float" by. Standout artists include Al Gromer Khan, Steve Roach, Robert Rich, and Gabrielle Roth and the Mirrors.

African
The polyrhythmic variances found throughout music styles from the African continent are fascinating, energizing, and invigorating. Popular favorites include Youssou N'Dour, Guem, and Mustapha Tettey.

American Classics
Longtime standards from such American composers and performers as Cole Porter, Scott Joplin, George and Ira Gershwin, Frank Sinatra, Sammy Davis Jr., Nat King Cole, and Tony Bennett.

Baroque
Rightfully associated with relaxation, this highly ornamental, spirited music is also very lively, bouncy, and uplifting. Composers from this

era, extending between 1600 and 1750, include Bach, Handel, Corelli, Vivaldi, Scarlatti, Telemann, and Pachelbel.

Big Band
This high-energy and lushly orchestrated dance music is typically associated with the 1930s and 1940s. It was performed by bands conducted by Artie Shaw, Count Basie, Benny Goodman, Duke Ellington, Glenn Miller, Woody Herman, and many others. This often-overlooked music is a big hit with many children—of all ages!

Bluegrass
"Bluegrass" generally refers to a type of highly entertaining, dance-oriented country music with religious undertones, originally popularized by Bill Monroe.

Broadway Show Music
This is music made popular by popular Broadway shows such as "Cats," "Annie," "Fiddler on the Roof," and hundreds of others. Broadway show tunes offer ample opportunities for dramatizations.

Celtic
Rapidly increasing in popularity, Celtic music brings together traditional folk and popular elements from the British Isles and has its roots in Celtic antiquity. Visions of kilts, Scottish moors, and medieval castles inspire spirited, exotic dances. This music ranges from highly dynamic and inspirational to very emotional and soothing.

Children's
Music for babies and children, designed for different stages of development. Children's music is broadly defined, and includes tunes from television shows (*Sesame Street*, *Barney*, *Ren and Stimpy*, *Pokemon*, *Teletubbies*) and films (Disney) as well as from such well-known artists as Joanie Bartels, Raffi, and Ella Jenkins. During the past few years, a number of popular artists have increased their involvement in creating children's music compilation albums, rapidly bridging the gap between old nursery rhymes and current popular music.

Classical

Although many people use the term "classical" to mean essentially all music written prior to the early 1900s, the word "Classical," with a capital C, refers to a period that involves the Viennese classics, and extends roughly between 1750 and 1820. This period essentially began with Haydn and Mozart, and extends to include early Beethoven and Schubert.

Country and Western

Visions of galloping horses and rodeos inspire children to "ride" and bounce with every beat. From cowboy salons to the Grand Ole Opry, country music will inspire children and their parents to join together in everything from two-stepping to line dancing. Performers from Jimmie Rodgers and Hank Williams to Shania Twain, Garth Brooks, and the Dixie Chicks have helped this music to evolve from its southern, rural roots to the worldwide influential sounds of today.

Drum and Percussion

From marches to ritual ceremonies to drum circles, drums and percussion continue to inspire the masses and bridge our cultural differences. Mickey Hart, David and Steve Gordon, Ottmar Liebert, and Brent Lewis are favorites.

Easy Listening

Contemporary music is usually orchestrated, instrumental versions of recent or current popular songs, produced for relaxation and background music.

Electronic

This term typically refers to the avant-garde-type music produced by the early pioneers of synthesizer music. Today it continues to be interesting because of its "complex simplicity." Major composers include Stockhausen, Varèse, and Babbitt.

Folk

Traditional ethnic music that reflects the mood, rhythms, and spirits of a newborn's ancestry is highly recommended to help introduce the cultural and ethnic collectivity of these sounds to our children.

Goth and Dark Ambient

This modern genre of dark, brooding music is heavily favored by teens and an increasing number of pre-teens who are struggling with repressed or unpleasant vibrations—whether feelings or thoughts— that are difficult to accept or process. The music tends to address these feelings and can have uplifting results. Also known as ethereal, esoteric, or occult music, the sounds are typically filled with hazy, obscure, and trance-inducing qualities.

Gothic Music

To differentiate from the above, this more traditional genre pertains to the period dating from about 1200 to 1450 A.D. and includes composers from Perotinus to Dufay.

Gospel

This term is typically associated with highly inspirational, stimulating, and uplifting religious popular music. Gospel has roots in Black and White spirituals, folk hymns, religious ballads, and other American secular folk songs.

House

This is essentially dance-club music, with strong beats and "raps," that is highly stimulating to many infants and young children as well as adults. Lyrical content is often questionable.

Jazz

A lot of the uninitiated think of jazz in the same vein as "Alternative." In reality, this truly American musical form can be as soothing, or as riveting, as the complex time signatures that extend through its tapestry of melodious and dissonant sounds. For high energy, Charlie Parker, Art Pepper, Miles Davis, and John Coltrane are recommended. For soothing sounds, Dexter Gordon, Ben Webster, and Ike Quebec are masters.

Latin, Calypso, and Reggae

This genre usually comprises "Island" music from the Caribbean, a lot of which is heavily influenced by African and Native American music.

Mediterranean

This music originated in the Middle East; today it fuses a variety of Mediterranean influences, contemporary and traditional music forms originating from Middle Eastern countries including Egypt, Israel, Turkey, Syria, Saudi Arabia, Iran, Iraq, and Yemen. Some popular, contemporary artists include Nusrat Fateh Ali Khan, Hamza El-Din, the Sabri Brothers, Amina Alaoui, and Hassam Hakmoun. A steady, growing interest in these musical styles has influenced Western artists ranging from Brian Jones (The Rolling Stones), Robert Plant and Jimmy Page (Led Zeppelin), to Peter Gabriel, Mickey Hart (The Grateful Dead), and Jeff Buckley.

Minimalism

Minimalist music is simple and repetitive, with little variation in melody or rhythm. Its effects range from relaxing to hypnotic or trance-like when properly produced. Pioneers include Philip Glass, Steve Reich, Robert Roach, George Winston, and John Adams.

Soundtracks

This music includes tunes from popular animated features as well as compilation tracks from popular artists and specifically orchestrated movie soundtracks. Children develop a strong affinity for movie-oriented music, as it is quickly associated with film scenes and commercial videos. Excellent soundtracks to children oriented films include *The Lion King* (Elton John and others), *The Adventures of Elmo in Grouchland* (various artists), *Tarzan* (Phil Collins), and the *Iron Giant* (various artists).

Native American

R. Carlos Nakai, Coyote Oldman, and Marina Raye are some of the artists bringing together these ancient, tribal rhythms that transport us into realms of trance-like relaxation, or enhanced alertness.

New Age

As with "Alternative" music, the term "New Age" has come to take innumerable guises and directions. "New Age" music can refer to any of several genres throughout this glossary, including Ambient,

Minimalism, Native American, Drum and Percussion, World, Electronic, Celtic, and Alternative.

Opera

Wagner, Verdi, Puccini, and Rossini are masters, but Mozart, Handel, and R. Strauss were also noted composers of opera. A music form for colossal voices or for acting out our innermost dramatic fantasies—preferably in the shower, or during long car rides in the mountains or out in the country.

Pop

It is easy to forget that "pop" simply stands for "*pop*ular" music. This is the top-40, mainstream music favored by most commercial stations.

Rap

Rap music is typically associated with inner city sounds and issues. It revolves around strong, rhythmic beats and rapid word rhymes. Lyrics often range from questionable to profane, with reference to violence and graphic sexuality. A lot of rap music, however, delivers very powerful, sensitive messages that are uplifting and even inspirational.

Renaissance

This music, which flourished between the early 1400s and 1600, is extremely colorful, invigorating, and uplifting, and usually gets children of all ages bouncing and dancing joyously. Composers from this area are not typical household names—unlike say, Mozart, Chopin, or Beethoven—and so music from this period is typically packaged in compilations reflecting the general Renaissance styles.

Rock

Pop that rocks.

Romantic

The Romantic music movement of the nineteenth century (roughly 1820 to 1880) followed the Classical period; it includes music ranging from Beethoven and Schubert to Tchaikovsky, Dvorak, Mahler, Strauss, and Holst. Music from this period, particularly piano music by composers such as Mendelssohn, Schumann, Chopin, Liszt, and Brahms, is often very appealing to children.

Rhythm and Blues
African-American music from the 40s to early 60s that evolved into "soul music." Founding stars include Ray Charles, Fats Domino, Jackie Wilson, and Etta James.

Soul
This term is usually reserved for the heartfelt, stirring music from African-American, 60s megastars such as The Temptations, Marvin Gaye, The Supremes, James Brown, Otis Redding, Aretha Franklin, Wilson Pickett, The Four Tops, Stevie Wonder, Sam and Dave, and others who recorded for such labels as Motown, Atlantic, and Stax.

South American
The various music types originating in South American countries usually borrow and blend sounds from African, European, Latin, and Native music styles and traditions.

Techno
A lot of children find the repetitive, trance-inducing effects of this type of music very stimulating. It often gets them bouncing and giggling in unbridled merriment. Use at your discretion! Techno-pop is a "milder" form of Techno music that is attractive to many pre-teens.

Waltzes
The brisk, animated nature of these dances in triple time is difficult to resist and quickly inspires children of all ages—and adults—to glide and prance across the floor as if touched by magical endorphins.

World
This label encompasses music from around the globe, but it typically describes music from the continents of Asia, India, Africa, and Australia. It can include many hybrid and cross-cultural influences.

Zydeco or Cajun
This music started out as the folk music of French-speaking residents of southwest Louisiana, and is influenced by Southern folk and rhythm and blues. It features fiddles, accordions, and even washboards, for tasty sounds to spice up many occasions.

Music Menu #29
Pop artists by the decade

The following is a list of popular groups and singers from various eras with excellent sing-along catalogs (many of these overlap across two or three decades).

Popular groups/singers from the 50s

Elvis	Ricky Nelson
The Platters	The Everly Brothers
Buddy Holly and The Crickets	Nat "King" Cole
Chuck Berry	Brenda Lee
Connie Francis	Jerry Lee Lewis
The Coasters	The Drifters

Popular groups/singers from the 60s

The Beatles	The Beach Boys
Herman's Hermits	The Monkees
The Temptations	The Supremes
Aretha Franklin	The Four Seasons
Three Dog Night	Creedence Clearwater Revival
Marvin Gaye	Stevie Wonder
The Rolling Stones	The Dave Clark Five

Popular groups/singers from the 70s

Paul McCartney	John Lennon
James Taylor	John Denver
Carole King	George Harrison
Michael Jackson	Elton John
Rod Stewart	Hall and Oates
The Eagles	Fleetwood Mac
The Carpenters	The Jackson Five
The Commodores	Donna Summer

Popular groups/singers from the 80s
(Parents should be sure to screen tunes before considering them for family sing-alongs)

Madonna	Lionel Ritchie
Cindy Lauper	Whitney Houston
Billy Joel	Duran Duran
Phil Collins	Huey Lewis and the News
New Kids on the Block	Bruce Springsteen
Olivia Newton John	Prince
Blondie	The Police

Popular groups/singers from the 90s
(Again, parents will want to screen the tunes)

Mariah Carey	Boyz II Men
Hanson	Backstreet Boys
The Spice Girls	All Saints
Salt-n-Pepa	Janet Jackson
Counting Crows	Ace of Base
Green Day	Alanis Morissette
Sheryl Crow	Smashing Pumpkins
Baby Face	Jewel
Britney Spears	The Dixie Chicks
Brandy	Goo Goo Dolls
TLC	'N Sync
Lauryn Hill	

Music Menu #30

Top 100 super-great all-time car sing-along oldies menu

ABC	The Jackson Five
All You Need Is Love	The Beatles
Baby Love	The Supremes
Bad Moon Rising	Creedence Clearwater Revival
Barbara Ann	The Beach Boys
Beat It	Michael Jackson
Billy Jean	Michael Jackson
Born in the USA	Bruce Springsteen
Can't You Hear My Heartbeat	Herman's Hermits
Crocodile Rock	Elton John
Daydream	The Lovin' Spoonful

Daydream Believer	The Monkees
Do You Believe in Magic	The Lovin' Spoonful
Don't Be Cruel	Elvis
Down on the Corner	Creedence Clearwater Revival
Downtown	Petula Clark
Ebony and Ivory	Paul McCartney and Stevie Wonder
Every Little Thing She Does Is Magic	The Police
Everyday	Buddy Holly
Free Fallin'	Tom Petty & The Heartbreakers
Fun, Fun, Fun	The Beach Boys
Gimme All Your Lovin'	ZZ Top
Girls Just Wanna Have Fun	Cindy Lauper
Gloria	Them (with Van Morrison)
Goin' Up the Country	Canned Heat
Good Vibrations	The Beach Boys
Grandma's Feather Bed	John Denver
Hanky Panky	Tommy James and The Shondells
Happy Together	The Turtles
Heart of Glass	Blondie
Henry the Eighth	Herman's Hermits
Hey Jude	The Beatles
High Hopes	Frank Sinatra
House at Pooh Corner	Loggins and Messina
I Get Around	The Beach Boys
I Heard It Through the Grapevine	Marvin Gaye
I Love Rock and Roll	Joan Jett & The Blackhearts
I Saw Her Standing There	The Beatles
I Think I Love You	The Partridge Family
I Want to Hold Your Hand	The Beatles
I Want You Back	The Jackson Five
I'm a Believer	The Monkees
I'm Into Something Good	Herman's Hermits
Isn't She Lovely	Stevie Wonder
It's My Party	Lesley Gore
Itsy Bitsy Teenie Weenie Yellow Polka Dot Bikini	Bryan Hyland
Johnny B. Goode	Chuck Berry

Joy to the World	Three Dog Night
Jump	Van Halen
Keep on Dancing	The Gentrys
King of the Road	Roger Miller
Knock Three Times	Tony Orlando and Dawn
Learning to Fly	Tom Petty & The Heartbreakers
Let's Go	The Cars
Let's Stay Together	Al Green
Love Shack	B-52's
Manic Monday	The Bangles
Margaritaville	Jimmy Buffett
Material Girl	Madonna
Mellow Yellow	Donovan
Mickey	Toni Basil
Mockin' Bird	James Taylor and Carly Simon
Mrs. Brown, You've Got a Lovely Daughter	Herman's Hermits
My Best Friend's Girl	The Cars
My Ding-a-Ling	Chuck Berry
My Girl	The Temptations
My Sharona	The Knack
Peaceful Easy Feeling	The Eagles
Peggy Sue	Buddy Holly
Proud Mary	Creedence Clearwater Revival
Reelin' and Rockin'	Chuck Berry
Respect	Aretha Franklin
Rock Around the Clock	Bill Haley and the Comets
Rockin' Robin	The Jackson Five
Rocky Mountain High	John Denver
Saturday Night	Bay City Rollers
Say, Say, Say	Paul McCartney and Michael Jackson
Shake Your Booty	KC and the Sunshine Band
She Loves You	The Beatles
Silly Love Songs	Paul McCartney
Simon Says	The 1910 Fruitgum Company
Speedy Gonzales	Pat Boone
Stop! In the Name of Love	The Supremes

Sugar Sugar	The Archies
Surfin' USA	The Beach Boys
Take Me Home Country Roads	John Denver
Takin' Care of Business	Bachman-Turner Overdrive
Taking It Easy	The Eagles
Teddy Bear	Elvis
That'll Be the Day	Buddy Holly
Twist and Shout	The Beatles
Uncle Albert/Admiral Halsey	Paul McCartney
Under the Boardwalk	The Drifters
Uptown Girl	Billy Joel
Walk Like an Egyptian	The Bangles
We're an American Band	Grand Funk Railroad
Y.M.C.A.	The Village People
Yellow Submarine	The Beatles
You're the One That I Want	Olivia Newton-John and John Travolta
Your Mamma Don't Dance	Loggins and Messina

Music Menu #31
Fifty selected children's music title reviews

The following CDs (and tapes) are strongly recommended to assist parents in meeting a number of their children's particular needs (stimulation, relaxation, education, inspiration) as well as in raising overall sound awareness.

Mothers to be: Mozart for Mothers to Be: Tender Lullabies for Mother and Child, from Set Your Life to Music Series. Gentle, soothing collection of moderately stirring Mozart pieces that weave a mosaic of peace and relaxation to relax both mom and baby-to-be.

High-energy/fun: Michael Anderson & The Polar Bear Band, by Same (toddlers to school-age). A lively, funny set including songs for both young and older children.

High-energy/silly/fun: Club Chipmunk: The Dance Mixes, by The Chipmunks (all ages). Cover versions of lively songs covering four decades (60s–90s) in the Chipmunks' fun, irresistible style.

High-energy/sing-along: Singable Songs for the Very Young, by Raffi (infants to preschoolers). Simply produced, well-known songs that will energize and appeal to young children who can sing along with the aid of the included lyrics.

High-energy/sing-along: Singing & Swinging, by Lois, Sharon and Bram (toddlers through school-age). Exquisite, generous assortment of active, entertaining songs designed for having a ball in the playroom.

High-energy. One World: One Light, by Nelson Gill (all ages). A mix of danceable, dynamic tunes in Caribbean style.

High-energy/sing-along: Cookin', by Ragy Rosen (toddlers to school-age). Upbeat, catchy collection of well-crafted children's tunes.

High-energy: Marooned on Tim's Island, by Tim Cain (toddlers to school-age). A sort of "Jimmy Buffet for children" assortment of fun and lively music.

High-energy/fun: Teaching Hippotami to Fly!, by The Chenille Sisters (toddlers to school-age). Mix of old and new upbeat songs that combine fun and laughter with entertaining messages.

High-energy/fun: Sing With the Animals, by various popular artists (all ages). Wonderful collection of pop songs, television theme songs and children's tunes brought to life by original and popular artists. A collection inspired by the cable channel Animal Planet.

High-energy/fun: Space Aliens, It's Party Time!, by Robbo (toddlers to school-age). Active pop tunes aimed at the trials and tribulations of preschoolers and young school-age children. Some parents will still be able to recall!

High-energy: Like a Ripple on the Water, by Kim & Jerry Brodey (preschoolers and older). Uplifting, energetic African-Latin rhythms with vibrant voices and multicultural messages.

Fun/party: You buy me!, by Tony Goldmark (school-age to preteen). Drawing from an eclectic array of musical styles, this collection is guaranteed to annoy parents but entertain children. Lives up to its title.

Fun/travel: A Child's Celebration of Folk Music, by various artists. (infants to preteen). Upbeat, amusing songs ranging from goofy ("There Ain't No Bugs on Me") through gushy ("World We Love"), to fun sing-alongs ("Riding in My Car") by famous artists.

Party/road: Doo-Wop Lollipops, by Stormy Weather (toddlers to school-age). Rock 'n' roll standards performed mostly a cappella in Doo-Wop style.

Silly/fun: Pinky & the Brain: Bubba Bo Bob Brain, by various artists (pre-schoolers and older). Pinky and the Brain's Animaniacs character involved in hilarious hi-jinks.

Silly/fun: Yakko's World, by Animaniacs (all ages). Zany collection of goofy tunes from the Animaniacs Cartoons.

Fun/sing-along: Jumpin' Up and Down, by Judy & David (toddlers through school-age). A funny bundle of catchy songs in diverse musical styles including creatively reworked standards with positive messages.

Fun/sing-along: Papa Chris Steve, by Papa Chris Major and Steve Farrell (toddlers through school-age). Bundle of catchy, melodious tunes that quickly become sing-alongs for preschool and some school-age children.

Holiday songs: Holiday Piggyback Songs, from Kimbo Educational (all ages). A rich compendium of holiday songs stretching across the entire spectrum from Thanksgiving, Kwanzaa, and Martin Luther King Day to Cinco de Mayo, Flag Day and the Chinese New Year!

Relaxation/eclectic: Return to Pooh Corner, by Kenny Loggins (all ages). Compilation of traditional and original tunes from well-known pop composers (Loggins, John Lennon, Paul Simon, Jimmy Webb, Rickie Lee Jones) sharing the theme of positive inspiration in a quieting mode.

Relaxation: Relax & Enjoy Your Baby, by Sylvia Klein Olkin (parents). Time-conscious, guided programs lasting five, ten and fifteen minutes designed specifically for busy expectant parents who need to take some time to recharge through relaxation and visualization exercises.

Relaxation: Dream Angels, by The Adelaide Symphony Orchestra (all ages). A calming array of classical and well-known contemporary selections that evoke peaceful atmospheres, calm moods, and restful states of mind.

Relaxation/lullabies: Love-A-Bytes: Quiet Songs of Love, by various artists (all ages). This compilation brings together songs that escort the listener (young or old) from relaxation, to contemplation, culminating in restful sleep.

Relaxation/lullabies: Love Songs & Lullabies for Daddy's Little Dreamer, by Tom Wurth (all ages). An impressive, heartfelt album from a male singer. Includes both sung and instrumental versions of original soothing songs.

Relaxation/lullabies: On a Starry Night, by Tracy & Thea Silverman (all ages). Excellent collection of multilingual, cross-cultural lullabies that set the stage for relaxing or drifting off to sleep.

Relaxation/lullabies: I Will Hold Your Tiny Hand, Steve Rashid (all ages). Superior collection of soothing songs and messages rendered in a heartwarming style by the artist. Highly recommended!

Relaxation/lullabies: Family Lullaby Classics: Billboard Presents, various artists (all ages). Fabulous compilation of popular film screen tunes by well-known artists bringing together a fresh blend of rarely considered lullabies.

Relaxation/lullabies: Lullaby: Tender Dreams, by Laura Nashman (young children). A superb combination of classical standards that range from relaxation and meditation to music to cradle both children and parents to a restful sleep.

Relaxation/bath: Baroque at Bathtime, by various artists (all ages). A Relaxing Serenade to Wash Your Cares Away (Set Your Life to Music series).

Lullabies: Billboard Presents: Family Lullaby Classics, by various popular artists (all ages). A superb package of popular artists performing soothing lullabies taken from classic films and musicals.

Lullabies: Lullaby: A Collection, by various artists (all ages). A delightful array of lullabies from renowned popular artists.

Bilingual relaxation/Lullabies: Lullabies of Latin America, by Maria Del Rey (all ages). As stated on the CD cover, this collection is "A Restful Little Heaven for You and Your Child." 14 Latin American "Canciones De Cuna," or "Crib Songs," are presented in both Spanish and English. A rich assortment of beautifully produced tunes.

Crosscultural lullabies/relaxation: A Legacy of Lullabies, and Lullabies & Love Songs, by Tanja Sonik (all ages). Sung in original Hebrew, Latino, and Yiddish, these volumes bring together a wealth of restful, meditative tunes.

Positive messages: Tia's Smile, by Tia (all ages). Inspired, original and updated songs that deliver positive messages to children of various ages.

Positive messages/fun: Cows and Other Assorted Fun Songs for Children, by Vince Junior (toddlers to school-age). Family-values tunes with universal themes presented through well-crafted, catchy tunes.

Positive messages/peer-oriented: Family Friendship Classics: Billboard Presents, various artists (school age and older). Wonderful compilation from the pop music archives that share the themes of friendship and the importance of relating to others.

Positive messages/world concepts: Peace Is the World Smiling, by various artists (all ages). Rare collection of message songs emphasizing peace, community, and caring for family and the environment.

Inspirational: When I Was a Child, by Anna Moo (all ages). Unique compilation of diverse original songs performed by Ms. Moo's distinctively sonorous voice. Inspiring enough to motivate budding songwriters to begin detailing their childhood events in musical-diary forms.

Eclectic: Nora's Room, by Jessica Harper (toddlers to school-age). Scintillating vocals, rich orchestration and versatile songs that draw from a number of diverse musical genres.

Eclectic: Reel Imagination: Classic Songs from Family Films, by Michele Nicastro (all ages). A rich, diverse collection of popular film tunes and 70s television sitcoms.

Eclectic: For Our Children, and *For Our Children Too*, by various popular artists (all ages). Two superb collections of well-known pop artists performing traditional children's and pop tunes.

Classics: AA! SSSha the Puppet, by Asha Putli (toddlers to school-age). A heartfelt interpretation of songs from Danny Kaye movies, including classics such as "The Ugly Duckling" and "Thumbelina."

Classic Showtunes: A Child's Celebration of Broadway, by original casts (all ages). Solid collection of original Broadway classics, with effects that appeal to children (and adults) of all ages.

Educational: Patchwork Quilt, by Peggo and Paul (all ages). A veritable time capsule of American history in song, this CD/tape is a "must have" for parents interested in sharing their cultural roots with their children.

Spanish: Canta Conmigo (Sing with Me), by Juanita Newland-Ulloa (toddlers to school-age). Sung in Spanish, these far-reaching songs provide a musical introduction to facilitating pronunciation through a fun, educational array of diverse tunes.

French: J'ai Tant Danse, by Carmen Campagne (toddlers to school-age). Upbeat, highly enjoyable songs in French that will inspire an introduction to pronunciation and exploration into this Romantic language.

Audio book: Irish Folk Tales for Children, by Sharon Kennedy (preschool to school age). Four enchanting Irish tales performed by Ms. Kennedy accompanied by Celtic instruments. Each captures the mind and triggers a mosaic of vivid imagery.

Story time: Fairytale Favorites in Story & Song, by Jim Weiss (preschoolers and older). A collection of excellently delivered fairy tales that emphasize poetic, rhythmic delivery with contemporary twists to well-known stories.

Environmental/positive: A Planet with One Mind, by Mike Pinder (preschoolers and older). A rich collection of mystifying songs with positive environmental messages wrapped in an enchanting musical package. Excellent!

APPENDIX B

GENERAL RESOURCES

The following books are recommended as resources for assisting parents with nurturing both their children and themselves.

1-2-3 Magic! Effective Discipline for Children 2-12. Thomas W. Phelan. Glen Ellyn, Ill.: Child Management, 1998.

Action Methods for Stress Management. Bobby Pfau. Dubuque, Iowa: Kendall-Hunt Publishing Co., 1999.

A Guy's Guide to Pregnancy: Preparing for Parenthood Together. Frank Mungeam. Hillsboro, Ore.: Beyond Words Publishing, 1998.

An Introduction to Music Therapy: Theory and Practice. William B. Davis, Kate E. Gfeller, and Michael H. Thaut. New York: McGraw-Hill, 1998.

Building Self-Esteem in Children. Patricia H. Berne and Louis M. Savary. New York: Crossroad Publishing Co., 1996.

Caring for Your Baby and Young Child: Birth to Age 5. The American Academy of Pediatrics. New York: Bantam Doubleday Dell Publishing, 1998.

Caring for Your School-Age Child: Ages 5 to 12. Edward L. Schor, editor. New York: Bantam Doubleday Dell Publishing, 1996.

Child Behavior: The Classic Childcare Manual from the Gessell Institute of Human Development. Frances L. Ilg, Louise Bates Ames, and Sidney M. Baker. New York: Harperperennial Library, 1992.

Childhood Stress. Eugene L. Arnold. New York: John Wiley and Sons, 1990.

Dealing With Anger. Marianne Johnston. Center City, Minn.: Hazelden Information and Educational Services, 1999.

Depression in the Young: What We Can Do to Help Them. Trudy Carlson. Duluth, Minn.: Benline Press, 1998

Emotionally Intelligent Parenting: How to Raise a Self-Disciplined, Responsible, Socially Skilled Child. Maurice Elias, Steven E. Tobias, and Brian S. Friedlander. New York: Harmony Books, 1999.

Helping Children Manage Stress: A Guide for Adults. James H. Humphrey. Washington, D.C.: Child Welfare League of America, 1998.

How Your Child Is Smart: A Life-Changing Approach to Learning. Dawna Markova with Anne Powell. Emeryville, Calif.: Conari Press, 1992.

Learn with the Classics: Using Music to Study Smart at Any Age. Ole Andersen, Marcy Marsh, and Arthur Harvey. Ukiah, Calif.: The Lind Institute, 1999.

Lonely, Sad and Angry: A Parent's Guide to Depression in Children and Adolescents. Barbara D. Ingersoll and Sam Goldstein. New York: Main Street Books, 1996.

Music Therapy Sourcebook. Cecilia Schulberg. St. Louis, Mo.: MMB Music Inc., 1986.

Nurturing Spirituality in Children: Simple Hands-On Activities. Peggy J. Jenkins. Hillsboro, Ore.: Beyond Words Publishing, 1995.

Parent as Mystic, Mystic as Parent. David Spangler. New York: Penguin, USA, 1998.

Parents as Mentors: A New Perspective on Parenting That Can Change Your Child's Life. Sandra C. Burt and Linda J. Perlis. Roseville, Calif.: Prima Publishing, 1999.

Protecting the Gift: Keeping Children and Teenagers Safe (and Parents Sane). Gavin de Becker. New York: Dial Press, 1999.

Raising a Daughter: Parents and the Awakening of a Healthy Woman. Jeanne Elium and Don Elium. Berkeley, Calif.: Ten Speed Press, 1994.

Raising a Happy, Unspoiled Child. Burton L. White. New York: Fireside, 1995.

Raising a Son: Parents and the Making of a Healthy Man. Don Elium and Jeanne Elium. Berkeley, Calif.: Celestial Arts, 1996.

Raising Happy Children: A Parent's Guide. Javad H. Kashani, Donna V. Mehregany, and Wesley D. Allen. New York: Three Rivers Press, 1999.

Raising Preschoolers: Parenting for Today. Sylvia B. Rimm and Katie Couric. New York: Random House, 1997.

Ready, Set, R.E.L.A.X.: A Research-Based Program of Relaxation, Learning and Self-Esteem for Children. Jeffrey S. Allen, Roger J. Klein, and Matthew Holden, Jr. Watertown, Wisc.: Inner Coaching, 1997.

The Relaxation and Stress Reduction Workbook, 4th Edition. Martha Davis, Elizabeth Robbins Eshelman, and Matthew McKay. Oakland, Calif.: New Harbinger Publications, 1998.

Rites of Passage: Celebrating Life's Changes. Kathleen Wall and Gary Ferguson. Hillsboro, Ore.: Beyond Words Publishing, 1998.

Self-Esteem: A Family Affair. Jean Illsley Clarke. Center City, Minn: Hazelden Information Educational Services, 1998.

Ten Days to Self-Esteem. David D. Burns. New York: Quill, 1993.

The Anger Workbook. Lorrainne Bilodeau. Minneapolis: CompCare Publications, 1992.

The Anxiety and Phobia Workbook, 2nd Edition. Edmund J. Bourne. Oakland, Calif.: New Harbinger Publications, 1995.

The Baby Book: Everything You Need to Know About Your Baby from Birth to Age Two. William Sears and Martha Sears. Boston: Little Brown and Co., 1993.

The Childhood Depression Sourcebook. Jeffrey A. Miller. Chicago: Lowell House, 1999.

The Confident Child: Raising Children to Believe in Themselves. A Compassionate, Practical Guide. T.E. Apter. New York: Bantam Doubleday Dell Publishing, 1998.

The Mozart Effect: Tapping the Power of Music to Heal the Body, Strengthen the Mind, and Unlock the Creative Spirit. Don G. Campbell. New York: Avon Books, 1997.

The Open Mind: Exploring the 6 Patterns of Natural Intelligence. Dawna Markova. Berkeley, Calif.: Conari Press, 1996.

The Tao of Music: Sound Psychology. John M. Ortiz. York Beach, Maine: Samuel Weiser, 1997.

What to Expect: The Toddler Years. Arlene Eisenberg, Heidi E. Murkoff, and Sandee E. Hathaway. New York: Workman Publishing, 1996.

When Kids Are Mad, Not Bad: A Guide to Recognizing and Handling Your Child's Anger. Henry A. Paul. New York: Berkley Publishing Group, 1999.

FAMILY-ORIENTED INTERNET WEB SITES

For parents (and children!)

Family Friendly Sites (Wealth of family-approved sites. Hundreds of links!) http://www.virtuocity.com/family.html

Family Internet (Nerve center for multitude of family-oriented sites) http://www.familyinternet.com

Parent Soup (Interactive, well-organized site with updated, helpful resources) http://www.parentsoup.com

ParenthoodWeb (Book reviews and information resource for parenting topics) http://www.parentsoup.com

Families Under Construction (Self-help site for families. Advice and resources) http://www.famucon.com

Single Parent's Association (Parenting tips, advice and support for single parents) http://www.singleparents.org

KidsSource Online (Educational and health care resource for parents and teachers) http://www.kidsource.com

SafeKids.Com (Safe-surfing kit with resources and information for families) http://www.safekids.com

SafeTeens.Com (Tips and information for parents and children who are learning to "surf") http://www.safeteens.com

AltaVista's Family Filter (Search engine—click on "Family Filter" for screening) http://altavista.com

Lycos Search Guard (Search engine with guard for parents to filter unwanted sites) http://www.personal.lycos.com/safetynet/ safetynet.asp

Go Network (Resource engine for family-oriented sites. Click on "GoGuardian") http://www.go.com

World Wide Web Music Resources page (Central location for Music on the Web) http://www.cecer.army.mil/~burnett/MDB/music Resources.html

Online Moms Webring (Center for parents to interact, share or submit web sites) http://www.geocities.com/Heartland/flats/1052/ onlinemoms.htm

Mom's Online (Advice and information for mothers on family issues. Hot tips, games) http://www.momsonline.com

Parenting Connection (Information, support, resources and activities for families) http://www.familyinternet.com/parenting/ parentingdestinations.html

Family Explorer (Science and nature activities for parents and children) http://www.webcom.com/safezone/FE/frame2.htm#MONTH

Child Development Institute (Parenting and child development information and resources) http://www.cdipage.com

Family Network (Advice, information and parenting resources) http://www.familynetwork.com

It's A Parent (Music specifically designed for use during pregnancy and childbirth) http://www.itsaparent.com

The Parent Institute (Parent involvement resources and links to family sites) http://www.parent-institute.com

American Medical Association KidsHealth Club (Medical and health information) http://www.ama.assn.org/KHClub

For children (and parents!)

Yahooligans! (Central location for tons of children and family-oriented resources) http://www.yahooligans.com

Disney Com Home Page (Wealth of family activities and resources from Disney) http://disney.go.com/home/homepage/today/html/index.html

Kid Pub WWW Publishing (Children can share stories, poetry and ideas) http://www.en-garde.com/kidpub

The Fourth R (Computer training programs for toddlers through teens) http://www.fourthR.com

Cyberkids (Music, games, art, a theater, chat and reading rooms for children) http://www.cyberkids.com

Kids Corner (Center for many child-oriented links and sites) http://www.familyinternet.com/kids/index/html

KiDiddles (Games, music, activities, a "mouse museum," and an online store for children) http://www.kididdles.com

Kidz Sing (Lyrics and music to children's and holiday songs. Great for sing-alongs) http://www.members.home.com/veeceet/index.html

Music World for Kids (An instructional site for basic music education for children) http://www.members.aol.com/muswrld/index.html

Lyrics World (Wonderful site for obtaining lyrics to sing-alongs) http://www.summer.com.br/~pfilho

Songs and rhymes of all nations (Tunes, lyrics and song samples from around the globe) http://www.mamalisa.com/world

Rock and Roll Hall of Fame (Web site for the Rock and Roll Hall in Cleveland, Ohio) http://www.rockhall.com

CBC 4 Kids (Information and resource center for parents and teachers) http://www.cbc4kids.ca

React (Webpage filled with information and resources for mature school children & teens) http://www.react.com

PURCHASING MUSIC THROUGH THE INTERNET

The following sites provide oodles of music reviews and titles spanning all available types, styles, and genres.

Children's Music Web: http://www.childrensmusic.org/index.html

Children's Music Web Guide: http://www.cowboy.net/~mharper/ Chmusiclist.html

Music for Little People: http://www.st6.yahoo.com/melody

eToys Music Store: http://www.etoys.com/html/em-home.shtml

Kathy's Music Links: http://www.island.net/~musicbox/ musiclinks.htm

The Basic Library of the World's Greatest Music (Classical music audio/video catalog) http://www.amusicworld.com

The following sites are useful for readers in Europe:

www.hmv.com
www.virginmega.com
www.tower.europe.com
www.amazon.co.uk/music
www.towerrecords.co.uk

MUSIC-RELATED ASSOCIATIONS

The Institute of Applied Psychomusicology
Dr. John M. Ortiz, *Founder and Director*
P.O. Box 113
Dillsburg, PA 17019

http://www.soundpsych.com
E-mail: Soundpsych@redrose.net
Institute offering Sound Psychology products, lectures, seminars, and workshops. Training and consulting services for schools, universities, businesses, mental health, social service, and parenting groups. Home for "The Soothing Pulse" CD and tape series.

Center for Music and Young Children
66 Witherspoon Street
Princeton, NJ 08542
(800) 728-2692
http://www.musictogether.com
Family-conscious programs for young children and music professionals.

MMB Music, Inc.
Contemporary Arts Building
3526 Washington Avenue
St. Louis, MO 63103-1019
(314) 531-9635
Resource center for music-related products.

The Woodwind & Brasswind Music Center
General Music Store
4004 Technology Drive
South Bend, IN 46628
(800) 348-5003
E-mail: Gms@wwandbw.com
Resource center for musical instruments and related products.

Accelerated Learning Systems
6193 Summit Trail
Norcross, GA 30092
(404) 446-3852
Resource center for music and related products.

LIND (Learning in New Dimensions) Institute
Ole Andersen, *President*
P.O. Box 14487
San Francisco, CA 94114
(415) 864-3396
    Institute for music resources, products, and lectures. Home for the "Relax with the Classics" CD series.

National Association for Music Therapy
505 Eleventh Street, S.E.
Washington, D.C. 20003
(202) 543-6864
    Programs and music-related resources for families and professionals.

The Open Ear Center
6717 N.E. Marshall
Bainbridge Island, WA 98110
(206) 842-5560
    Center for music-related resources, lectures, and seminars.

The Mozart Effect
Don Campbell, *Founder*
P.O. Box 4719
Boulder, CO 80306
(303) 440-8046
    Resource center for the Mozart Effect products and lectures.

American Music Therapy Association
8455 Colesville Road, Suite 930
Silver Spring, MD 20910
(301) 589-3300
http://www.musictherapy.org
    National music therapy educational programs and music resources.

Kindermusik International
P.O. Box 26575
Greensboro, NC 27415
(800) 628-5687
    Educational courses designed for preschool children.

The Children's Group
1400 Bayly Street # 7
Pickering, ON L1W 3R2
Canada
(800) 668-0242
    Classical music resources.

MUSIC-RELATED RESEARCH JOURNALS AND PUBLICATIONS

The Arts in Psychotherapy
Elsevier Science Inc.
665 Avenue of the Americas
New York, NY 10010

Journal of Music Therapy
8455 Colesville Road, Suite 930
Silver Spring, MD 20910

Psychomusicology: A Journal of Research in Music Cognition
Center for Music Research
Florida State University
Tallahassee, FL 32306

The Psychology of Music
Department of Psychology
The University, Leicester
LE1 7RH, UK (England)

International Journal of Arts Medicine
MMB Music, Inc.
Contemporary Arts Building
3526 Washington Avenue
St. Louis, MO 63103

International Arts Medicine Association Newsletter
714 Old Lancaster Road
Bryn Mawr, PA 19010

Open Ear Journal
6717 N.E. Marshall Road
Bainbridge Island, WA 98110

Music Therapy Perspectives
American Music Therapy Association
8455 Colesville Road, Suite 930
Silver Spring, MD 20910

Rhythm Music Magazine
872 Massachusetts Avenue 2-7
Cambridge, MA 02139

Popular Music and Society
Popular Press
Bowling Green State University
Bowling Green, OH 43403

Music Educators Journal
1806 Robert Fulton Drive
Reston, VA 22091

APPENDIX C

A MUSICAL DAY IN THE LIFE OF...

The purpose of the following charts is to provide parents with time-efficient ways of raising sound awareness and introducing music, and sound, into each day.

Busy parents (are there any other kind?!) can raise sound awareness in a number of ways that do not have to impinge on their already overwhelming schedules. As a matter of fact, parents themselves can take advantage of music to help them relax, become energized, let go of nagging concerns, clear their minds, and become centered (see chapter 12).

"Musical days" involve more than simply playing music you and your children enjoy—"musical days" take advantage of all the sound vibrations that abound in our world and affect us in everyday life.

The following suggestions are provided as ideas that parents can choose from on a daily basis to help raise their children's sound awareness. Designed to fit into any "time budget," the suggestions below require time ranging from only a few seconds (making a positive, supportive comment) to a few minutes (singing a song or two), to hours (going on a Sound Safari!). The amount of preparation for these suggestions can also range from none at all (giving supportive feedback and encouragement when appropriate), to a few minutes (finding a proper CD to play at nap, dinner, or bubble-bath time), to a few hours (preparing the house for a musical party).

A Musical Day in the Life of...
... all children!

Throughout the day, and with every opportunity:

- First and foremost, listen—to your children and to yourself (see chapter 3).

- Respect your children's opinions and ideas. Children often remind us of thoughts and feelings we have long forgotten or have learned to block out.
- Give positive feedback, encouragement, and praise.
- Help to enrich your children's vocabularies by teaching them new words (see chapter 2, and Music Menus 3, 4, 5, and 6).
- Explain new concepts clearly and in terms your children understand (see chapter 3).

Sound Suggestion

Turn to: "Intermission: Top Ten Hits of Sound Awareness" on page 89, and "Encore! Growing Children" on page 175, for additional ideas.

Morning

A Musical Day in the Life of...
...an infant

- Play soft music for your new baby throughout the morning (see Music Menus 14 and 23).
- Shower your infant with comforting, positive messages of love and support (see chapters 3 and 7, and Music Menu 18).
- Help your baby's speech development by speaking directly, softly, and confidently (see chapters 2 and 3).
- Encourage your baby to copy, mimic, and echo your sounds (see chapters 2 and 3).
- Encourage your baby to play with sound-producing and musical toys (see chapter 5).

A Musical Day in the Life of...
...a toddler

- Welcome your child to each day with warm, comforting messages (see Intermission, Encore!, and chapters 3 and 7).
- Help to strengthen your child's self-identity with the aid of musical (see Music Menu 18) and nurturing messages (see Intermission, Encore!, and chapters 3 and 7).

- Point out unusual sounds to help your child develop an interest in, and awareness of, sounds in general (see chapter 3).
- Verbally acknowledge the positive strides your child makes each day (see chapter 3).
- Choose a new word each day, and encourage your child to use it throughout the day in different situations (see chapters 2 and 3).

A Musical Day in the Life of...
... a preschool child

- Welcome your child to each day with a warm, comforting message (see Intermission, and chapters 3 and 7).
- Help to strengthen your child's self-identity with the aid of musical (see Music Menu 18) and nurturing messages (see Intermission, Encore!, and chapters 3 and 7).
- Point out at least one of your child's good qualities each day (see chapter 2).
- Ask your child to name his favorite sound of the day, or his favorite word for the day, and to tell you why it's a favorite (see chapter 2).

A Musical Day in the Life of...
... a school-age child

- Welcome your child to each day with a warm, comforting message (see Intermission, and chapters 3 and 7).
- Help to strengthen your child's self-identity with the aid of musical (see Music Menu 18) and nurturing messages (see Intermission, Encore!, and chapters 3 and 7).
- Each day, acknowledge your child with positive feedback for something attempted or accomplished (see Encore!).
- As your child prepares for school each day, ask her to choose a "word for the day." The word can be a reminder of something in particular, or just one that has a certain agreeable sound, meaning, or quality.
- As your child arrives home from school, ask him to tell you about a particularly interesting sound he may have heard during the day.

Afternoon

A Musical Day in the Life of...
... an infant

- Play stimulating music when you play with your child (see Music Menus 16 and 31).
- Expose your baby to different types of musical styles (see Music Menus 8, 20, 21, 23, 24, and 31) throughout the day.
- Encourage your baby to experiment with various pitches, tones, and other sounds (see chapter 2).
- Take your favorite music along when you take your baby for a stroll.
- Take a few minutes once or twice a week to expose your baby to a new tune or two. Reinforce these tunes throughout the week, by either singing or playing them, as part of your daily interactions (see Music Menus 5 and 31).

A Musical Day in the Life of...
... a toddler

- Include some music- and sound-producing toys in your child's toy budget and encourage her to use them by asking her to "teach" you about the toy and sounds (see chapter 5).
- Expose your toddler to different types of musical styles (see Music Menus 8, 20, 21, 23, 24, 28, and 31).
- Try to include your child in part of your physical workouts. Use music to animate your routines and set your pace (see Music Menu 15).
- Take a few minutes once or twice a week to teach your child a tune or two. Rehearse those tunes together throughout the week as part of your daily play time (see Music Menus 5 and 7).
- Make relaxation part of your child's daily routine. Make a tradition of having your child set aside a ten- to fifteen-minute period solely for music-accompanied relaxation every day (see chapter 4 and Music Menu 14. Depending on your child's temperament, you may need to start with five-minute periods and work up from there).
- Take advantage of music to help introduce your toddler to various academic subjects and to trigger interest in the pursuit of learning (see chapters 2 and 3, and Music Menus 8 through 13 and 21).

A Musical Day in the Life of...

...a preschool child

· Allow opportunities for your child to experiment with musical instruments (see chapter 2).

· Expose your young child to different types of musical styles (see Music Menus 8, 20, 21, 23, 24, and 31).

· Include your child in your physical workouts. Use this opportunity to teach your child how to choose music for the purpose of exercise (see Music Menu 15).

· Make relaxation part of your child's daily routine. Begin a tradition of having your child set aside a fifteen- to twenty-minute period solely for music-accompanied relaxation every day (see chapter 4 and Music Menu 14. Depending on your child's temperament, you may need to start with five-minute periods and work up from there).

· Take advantage of music to help expand your preschooler's academic curiosity and knowledge (see chapters 2 and 3, and Music Menus 8 through 13 and 21).

A Musical Day in the Life of...

...a school-age child

· Encourage your child to pursue musical activities in school (see chapter 9).

· Encourage exploration with at least one musical instrument (see chapter 2).

· Make relaxation part of your child's daily routine. Begin a tradition of having your child set aside a twenty-minute period solely for music-accompanied relaxation every day (see chapter 4 and Music Menu 14. Depending on your child's temperament, you may need to start with five-minute periods and work up from there). A good time for school-age children to practice relaxation is when they arrive home from school and need to unwind and recharge.

· Help to support your child's scholarly and academic pursuits with the aid of music (see Music Menus 8 through 13 and 21).

Evening

A Musical Day in the Life of...
... an infant

- Play bubble-bath tunes during bathtime (see chapter 8 and Music Menu 22).
- Play soothing background music as you rock, nurse, or feed your child (see chapters 2 and 4, and Music Menus 14 and 17).
- Create nurturing sound environments throughout your home (see chapter 10).
- Do not play loud or stimulating music within thirty minutes of your baby's bedtime.
- End each day with comforting words (see Intermission and chapter 7).
- Escort your child to sleep with soothing music (see chapter 6 and Music Menu 17).

A Musical Day in the Life of...
... a toddler

- At least once a week, share fifteen minutes of musical time with your toddler (see chapters 4, 5, 9, and 10).
- Once or twice a week, play a musical game or activity (see chapter 9).
- Create nurturing sound environments throughout your home (see chapter 10).
- Consider playing soothing music as part of a new family tradition at least once or twice per week (see chapter 10).
- Set aside time for your child to listen to audio books at least once a week (see Music Menu 13). Choose audio books recommended for your child's age (see Music Menu 10).
- Take time out, at least once a week, to teach your child the words to a song (see Music Menus 5, 6, 7, 19, 20, 21, and 23).
- Do not play, or allow your child to listen to, loud or stimulating music within thirty minutes of his or her bedtime.
- End each day with a positive, nurturing, and comforting message (see chapter 7).
- Escort your child to sleep with soothing music (see chapter 6 and Music Menu 17).

A Musical Day in the Life of...
...a preschool child

- Create nurturing sound environments throughout your home (see chapter 10).
- Consider playing soothing music as part of a new family tradition at least once or twice per week (see chapter 10).
- Set aside time for your child to listen to audio books at least once a week (see Music Menu 13).
- Take time out, at least once a week, to sit down with your child and learn the words to a song together (see Music Menus 5, 6, 19, 20, and 23).
- Do not play, or allow your child to listen to, loud or stimulating music within thirty minutes of her or his bedtime.
- End each day with a positive, nurturing, and comforting message (see chapter 7).
- Assist your child in selecting soothing music to settle into a good night's rest (see chapter 6 and Music Menus 14, 23, and 31).

A Musical Day in the Life of...
...a school-age child

- Create nurturing sound environments throughout your home (see chapter 10).
- Consider playing soothing music as part of a new family tradition at least once or twice per week (see chapter 10).
- Encourage your child to tell you about a current favorite tune, or a song he or she has learned recently, as a regular tradition—for instance, one song per week (see chapter 3).
- Do not play, or allow your child to listen to, loud or stimulating music within thirty minutes of his or her bedtime.
- End each day with a positive, nurturing, and comforting message (see chapter 7).
- Monitor your child's musical leanings and encourage the playing of peaceful, calming music when bedtime approaches (see chapter 6 and Music Menus 14, 23, 28, and 31).

Weekends

Infants

- At least once a month, take your child to a musical activity—a religious function, concert, play, or other musical performance.
- Shelter your baby from loud music and noisy places.
- Whenever the weekends allow a few extra minutes of free time, take advantage of these opportunities to explore nature and musical sounds with your baby (see chapter 2).

Toddlers

- At least once a month, take your child to a musical activity—a religious function, concert, play, or other musical performance.
- Encourage and support your child's participation in organized musical functions, whether through playing an instrument, singing, or becoming otherwise involved in the activity.
- Shelter your young child from loud music and noisy places.
- At least once every couple of weeks, engage your family in musical games and activities (see chapter 9).
- Take your child on a Sound Safari two or three times a year (see chapter 9).
- Make road trips a musical experience (see chapter 10, and Music Menus 5, 7, 19, 20, 25, 26, 30, and 31).
- Once a month, arrange a music-oriented party for your children and their friends (see chapter 9, and Music Menus 16, 23, 24, 25, and 31).
- Teach your children about household chores with the aid of music (see chapter 11 and Music Menu 16).
- Expand your family's new musical traditions to include your children's grandparents, other relatives, and family friends (see chapters 8 and 9).
- Introduce your child to the Internet by searching, and exploring, various music Web sites (see Family-Oriented Internet Web Sites in Appendix B).
- Take advantage of the many family-oriented music software packages, CDs, and other computer-related musical possibilities as part of your computer learning and teaching experiences (see Family-Oriented Internet Web Sites in Appendix B).

Preschool-age children

- At least once a month, take your child to a musical activity—a religious function, concert, play, or other musical performance or activity.
- Encourage your child to participate in organized musical functions, whether through playing an instrument, singing, or becoming otherwise involved in the activity.
- At least once every couple of weeks, engage your family in musical games and activities (see chapter 9).
- Make road trips a musical experience (see chapter 10, and Music Menus 7, 19, 20, 25, 26, 29, 30, and 31).
- Take your child on a Sound Safari once or twice every few months (see chapter 9).
- A couple of times a year, take the family for a tour to a musical site, such as the birthplace of a famous musician, a music hall, or a museum of musical instruments.
- Take advantage of timely opportunities to introduce your child to your musical past (see chapter 8 and Music Menu 29).
- Take advantage of timely opportunities to learn about your child's preferred music (see chapter 3 and Music Menu 31).
- Take time once in a while to learn about different types of music so that you are able to make informed choices when selecting music and teaching your child about various contemporary—or classical—styles (see Music Menus 21, 28, 29, and 31).
- Take time out during the weekend to teach, or play for, your child, an old song that was popular when you were his or her age (see Music Menu 29).
- Include music as part of your family's housecleaning tradition (see chapter 11 and Music Menu 16).
- Expand your family's new musical traditions to include your children's grandparents, other relatives, and family friends (see chapters 8 and 9).
- With your child, learn to navigate and explore the Internet by searching and exploring various music Web sites (see Family-Oriented Internet Web Sites in Appendix B).

· Take advantage of the many family-oriented music software packages, CDs, and other computer-related musical possibilities as part of your computer learning and teaching experiences (see Family-Oriented Internet Web Sites in Appendix B).

School-age children

· At least once a month, take your child to a musical activity—a religious function, concert, play, or other musical performance or activity.

· Encourage your child to participate in organized musical functions, whether through playing an instrument, singing, or becoming otherwise involved in the activity.

· At least once every couple of weeks, engage your family in musical games and activities (see chapter 9).

· Make road trips a musical experience (see chapter 10 and Music Menus 7, 19, 26, 30, and 31).

· A couple times a year, take the family for a tour to a musical site, such as the birthplace of a famous musician, a music hall, or a museum of musical instruments.

· Take your child and a friend on a Sound Safari at least once a year (see chapter 9).

· Escort your child (and a friend) to a pop music concert.

· Take advantage of timely opportunities to introduce your child to your musical past (see chapter 8 and Music Menu 29).

· Take advantage of timely opportunities to learn about your child's preferred music (see chapter 3 and Music Menu 31).

· Take time once in a while to learn about different types of music so that you are able to make better informed choices when selecting music and teaching your child about various contemporary—or classical—styles (see Music Menus 21, 28, 29, and 31).

· Use music to help motivate your children, and yourself, during household chores (see chapter 11 and Music Menu 16).

· Expand your family's new musical traditions to include your children's grandparents, other relatives, and family friends (see chapters 8 and 9).

- Take advantage of your child's proficiency with the Internet by encouraging her or him to teach you how to search for, and utilize, the many interesting music Web sites available (see Family-Oriented Internet Web Sites in Appendix B).
- Take advantage of the many family-oriented music software packages, CDs, and other computer-related musical possibilities as part of your computer learning and teaching experiences (see Family-Oriented Internet Web Sites in Appendix B).

Holidays

All ages

- Make music a part of your family holiday traditions (see chapter 9 and Music Menu 27).
- Make family vacations a musical experience (see chapter 10 and Music Menus 19, 26, and 30).
- Take advantage of family gatherings during holidays to help your children explore their family ancestry through music (see chapter 8 and Music Menu 29).
- As you travel during holiday time, take music along for the ride (see chapter 10 and Music Menus 7, 19, 20, 25, 26, 29, 30, and 31).
- Take some time during homebound holidays to upgrade the musical ambience throughout your home (see chapter 10).

Planning ahead. To further maximize your time during the week, take some time during the weekend to set aside a number of selections you'd like to play later. Keep them close to your sound system. If your family owns a multi-play CD player, you can load the CDs for the week (or the month!) all at one time. That way, when the need for music beckons, all you need to do is push a button!

Morning

Awaken to a sound day. Begin each day by waking to pleasant music.

Scramble up some positive vibes. Embellish your family breakfast with moderately upbeat, lively tunes. The style or type of music is irrelevant. The feeling is what is important.

Too cool for school. Play music as you drive your child to school, or yourself to work—soothing music to calm down, moderately stimulating music to awaken the senses.

Afternoon

Nurturing soundtracks. Houseparents benefit by playing music to help with their daily chores. Lively, up-tempo music played at moderate volumes can help to stimulate both work and creativity.

Naptime music. For naptimes, enhance your child's restful sleep with some of the many lullaby compilations available.

Time managing. Use a tape or CD to help regulate your child's naptime. When the music is over, you will know that naptime is over as well.

Parent naptime. Coordinate naptime with meditation or relaxation time for yourself. Use a relaxation tape or CD, such as "The Soothing Pulse." (For information on "The Soothing Pulse" CD or tape, please refer to The Institute of Applied Psychomusicology under Music-Related Associations in Appendix B.) It is specifically designed to provide maximum relaxation and "recharging" of one's resources in a short period of time.

Playtime. Complement and enhance daily playtime with the aid of selective music backgrounds. Browse through the Music Menu sections throughout this book for musical ideas to fit almost every occasion.

Study/reading time. Some types of soft, soothing music have been found to encourage and improve a number of academic skills. Turn to the music menus for some sound suggestions.

Clean-up time. Use music as a motivating background tool to stimulate your child (and yourself) as you join forces to clean up the house or yard. Lively, stimulating, upbeat music is best for this task.

Evening

Glad to head home. Play music on the way back home. Relax and unwind with soft music.